Manchester Hidden Walks

Jonathan Schofield

For my brother Charles, a true Lancastrian;
humour, grit, ever curious about the world.

Published by Geographers'
A-Z Map Company Limited
An imprint of HarperCollins Publishers
Westerhill Road
Bishopbriggs
Glasgow
G64 2QT

HarperCollinsPublishers
Macken House, 39/40 Mayor Street Upper,
Dublin 1, D01 C9W8, Ireland

www.az.co.uk
a-z.maps@harpercollins.co.uk

1st edition 2023

Text and routes © Jonathan Schofield
Mapping © Collins Bartholomew Ltd 2023

This product uses map data licenced from
Ordnance Survey© Crown copyright and
database rights 2022 OS 100018598

AZ, A-Z and AtoZ are registered trademarks
of Geographers' A-Z Map Company Limited

A catalogue record for this book
is available from the British Library.

ISBN 978-0-00-856494-0

10 9 8 7 6 5 4 3

Printed in India

This book contains FSC™ certified paper and other controlled
sources to ensure responsible forest management.

For more information visit: www.harpercollins.co.uk/green

contents

introduction

Manchester is flesh and blood and bricks and mortar but it is also a concept, an idea. Historians, novelists and visitors have noted this for two centuries since it became the emblem of the social changes of the Industrial Revolution just as much as it did for the metamorphosis wrought by manufacturing, science and commercial innovation. In the late twentieth century Manchester became a symbol again, a byword for the decline typical of so many of the big British cities away from the capital.

Its recent regeneration – the way the skyline has rocketed to the heavens, the massive increase in the central population, the growth in amenity – has made it a magnet for those studying urban renewal in Europe. Yet, as you will see on these walks, especially the tour through east Manchester, regeneration has not spread evenly. In 1997, Jim McClellan wrote, 'Manchester's size […] makes the social processes more visible. You can see how things are developing. Where they might end up is another matter.'

Exactly. This book will underscore so many contemporary British urban themes as we tour through the physical city and its neighbour Salford, but also excursion through the metaphysical realm of people and ideas. Chocolate box Manchester is not, and it is so much the better for that. Of course, we have Chetham's in the city centre, the Delph at Worsley and the Old Parsonage in Didsbury, but we also have MECD at the University, Deansgate Square and Afflecks. Manchester is old and new, charm and tough bones, silly and serious, a lexicon of architecture good and bad, drama everywhere for those with eyes to see. All of this is best enjoyed through the soles of your shoes. Go on, walk some Manchester, feel it.

about the author

Jonathan Schofield is a tour guide and writer with several books to his name. He was awarded the University of Manchester's Medal of Honour for services to the city in 2021. He has appeared on several TV and radio broadcasts including *Great British Railway Journeys*, *Britain's Most Historic Cities*, *The Matter of the North* and *No Place Like Home*. Manchester and North West England is his home, his identity.

how to use this book

Each of the 20 walks in this guide
is set out in a similar way.
They are all introduced with a brief
description, including notes on
things you will encounter on your
walk, and a photograph of a place
of interest you might pass along
the way.

On the first page of each walk there
is a panel of information outlining
the distance of the walk, a guide
to the walking time, and a brief
description of the path conditions

or the terrain you will encounter.
A suggested starting point along
with the nearest postcode is shown,
although postcodes can cover
a large area therefore this is just
a rough guide.

The major part of each section
is taken up with route maps and
detailed point-to-point directions
for the walk. The route instructions
are prefixed by a number in a circle,
and the corresponding location is
shown on the map.

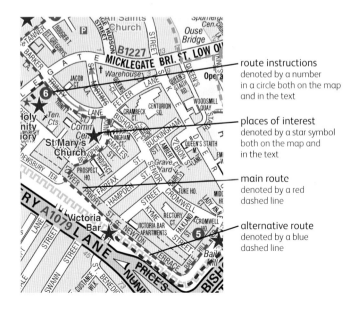

route instructions
denoted by a number
in a circle both on the map
and in the text

places of interest
denoted by a star symbol
both on the map and
in the text

main route
denoted by a red
dashed line

alternative route
denoted by a blue
dashed line

A-Z walk one

Civic Grandeur

Impressive buildings in the city centre.

The area around St Peter's Square and Albert Square contains some of the most monumental buildings in Manchester. It's an easy area to walk, having lots of public space and pedestrianized roads.

This short circular walk takes in Central Library, the Town Hall Extension, the former Free Trade Hall, Manchester Central and many other extraordinary Manchester buildings. One of the greatest civic UK buildings is included, Manchester Town Hall, which opened in 1877 and is often called 'a classic of its age'. You will also pass a church containing a remarkable series of paintings that shock by being so at odds with the rest of the interior.

The key is to look up as you walk round these parts, except when crossing roads of course, to take full advantage of the details on the buildings and appreciate the range of architectural styles and periods. You will find deep historical resonances with tributes to an American president and the leader of the women's suffrage movement in the UK, not to mention big moments in musical history. This walk also takes in a melancholy monument to one of the great tragedies in British history that took place in this area during the struggle for democracy.

start / finish	St Peter's Square
nearest postcode	M2 5PD
distance	1 mile / 1.5 km
time	40 minutes
terrain	Paved roads and paths.

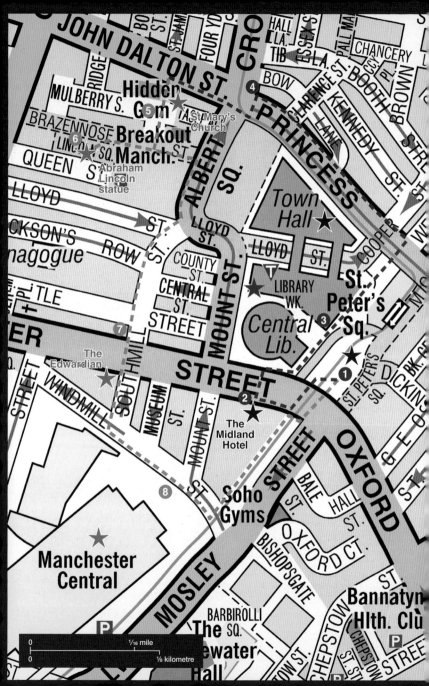

1 Start in St Peter's Square ★ , at the commemorative cross by ecclesiastical architect Temple Moore. The cross marks where St Peter's Church stood until demolished in 1907 to help create the square. The design of the church is etched in the pavement slabs. Cross the tram lines towards the round building with columns, Central Library. Across the road is the large terracotta structure of The Midland Hotel ★ , built for the Midland Railway Company in 1903 by Charles Trubshaw. Cross Peter Street to see a ceramic relief of Rolls and Royce under the hotel's entrance arches. They met here in 1904 to start their motor company. Henry Royce was the Manchester manufacturer and Charles Rolls the salesman.

2 Cross back over Peter Street and walk past the front of Central Library, which references the Pantheon in Rome but rather than being a temple to all the gods, this is a temple to all human knowledge. It opened in 1934 and remains a stunning civic success: before the Covid-19 pandemic, it was the most popular library in the UK, with 1.6 million readers. The architect was Vincent Harris. The building opens long hours so a trip up to the domed and round main reading room is rewarding, though beware its locally famous echo. Over to your right, between two modern office blocks on the other side of the tram lines, is Hazel Reeves' statue of Emmeline Pankhurst, the Mancunian leader of the Suffragettes. It was erected in 2018 on the anniversary of women gaining the vote in Britain.

3 Facing Central Library, turn right through the arcade of the Town Hall Extension. This is from 1936, also by Vincent Harris. On the St Peter's Square side the tall gable carries shields representing England and Scotland, on the Mount Street side those of Ireland and Wales. Follow the arcade and you arrive at Manchester's cenotaph, designed by Sir Edwin Lutyens. Cross Princess Street and turn left past the Waterhouse pub with Manchester Town Hall on the left.

4 Ignoring the Town Hall for now, cross at the lights to the left side of John Dalton Street. John Dalton was hugely celebrated in Manchester as the father of atomic theory and the man who first described colour blindness. He died in 1844 by which time he'd donated his eyeballs to science: they still reside in the Science and Industry Museum if you want a peep at his peepers. Just before the Ape and Apple pub, turn left into Dalton Passage and follow it to St Mary's Church ★ , the city centre's Roman Catholic place of worship (the RC Cathedral is over the river in Salford). St Mary's is a Romanesque-style church from 1848. It has an elaborate marble interior made all the better by the clash with some of the most remarkable paintings of the Stations of the Cross by Norman Adams from 1994.

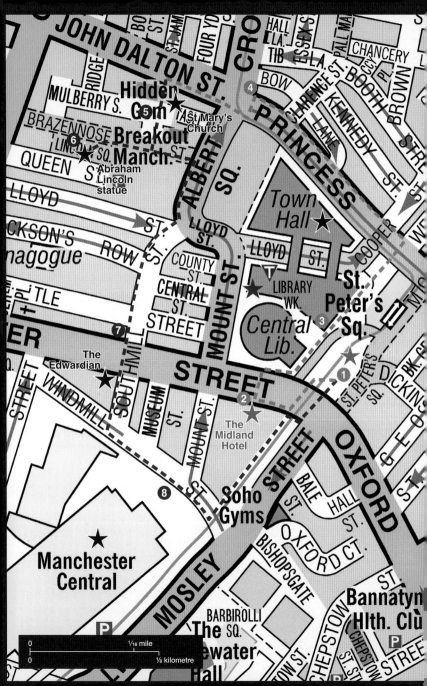

5 Continue to Brazennose Street and turn right into Lincoln Square, named for the larger-than-life Abraham Lincoln statue ★ by George Grey Barnard. The statue was gifted to the city by grateful Americans for the support Manchester and southeast Lancashire gave the Union in the American Civil War. This support came despite the hardship the Civil War caused in Lancashire as the cotton failed to arrive and work dried up. When Lincoln was assassinated, the only letters found on his body were from former Manchester MP, John Bright.

6 Retrace your steps but carry straight on rather than turning left to St Mary's and you arrive at Albert Square. If the full refurbishment of the area is complete you will see the square dominated by the neo-Gothic Town Hall ★. Opened in 1877 and designed by Alfred Waterhouse, it is a masterpiece inside and out. The building has an 85-metre (280-foot) clock tower which is crowned by a large golden ball with spikes representing a cotton boll and also the sun, an arrogant symbol of 'wherever the sun shines Manchester has influence'. Dominating the square is the Albert Memorial by Thomas Worthington, later copied in London's Hyde Park. Leave Albert Square by Southmill Street for Peter Street.

7 Over the road here is The Edwardian hotel ★, formerly Free Trade Hall, perhaps the only UK building named after an economic philosophy. This was the home of debates, school and college prize-givings, political rallies, boxing bouts, theatre, indeed anything went. The Italianate facade by Edward Walters is all that survives from the original 1856 building, the rest destroyed in the 1940 Christmas Blitz. Rebuilt, it hosted many gigs and in 1976, with an appearance of the Buzzcocks, kickstarted Manchester's indie music scene. It was converted into a hotel in 1996. Continue over Peter Street on Southmill Street to the left of the Edwardian Hotel and turn left to the canopy of Manchester Central ★.

8 Manchester Central is the exhibition centre for the city and was a former railway station, originally opening in 1880. Inside it has 10,000 square metres of uninterrupted space. It has held important gigs as well as exhibitions and political conferences. On one side of the forecourt is an unusual circular and stepped monument marking the Peterloo Massacre. About 50,000 to 80,000 people had gathered in open ground here on 16 August 1819 to protest about a lack of representation and a lack of the vote. Eighteen people died when attacked by the local amateur soldiers, the yeomanry. It was a key moment on the road to UK democracy. Two years later *The Manchester Guardian*, now *The Guardian*, was first published, in many respects a result of Peterloo. Continue to the end of Windmill Street then turn left to follow the tramlines back to the start point.

A̅Z̲ walk two

Cottonopolis

A meander through the commercial district.

Manchester used to be internationally famous as a textile city, although it was always a more complicated city scene than just one of cotton, as this route shows. It might start off with the emblematic building of the vast cotton industry at the Royal Exchange but then takes an entertaining diversion into the former banking heart of Manchester, 'the half square mile'.

You pass associations with a famous newspaper, a curious 'ginnel', grand commercial buildings, a library, a pre-industrial 'cottage', finishing with art and a specific Manchester building type.

As the proto-industrial powerhouse, the city became as much a symbol as a place of bricks and mortar and flesh and blood. The first city to industrialize in every nation was almost always nicknamed the 'Manchester' of that nation, thus Osaka in Japan, Ahmedabad in India, Chemnitz in Germany, Norrkoping in Sweden and so on.

There are pre-industrial links on this walk, with the windows of one building telling its own story, while a famous Greater Manchester artist permanently sups in what was his favourite pub. Remember, keep looking above the first floor of buildings to see delights in this elaborate part of commercial Manchester.

start	Royal Exchange, Cross Street
nearest postcode	M2 7DH
finish	Junction of Princess Street and Portland Street
distance	¾ mile / 1.1 km
time	40 minutes
terrain	Paved roads, some steps.

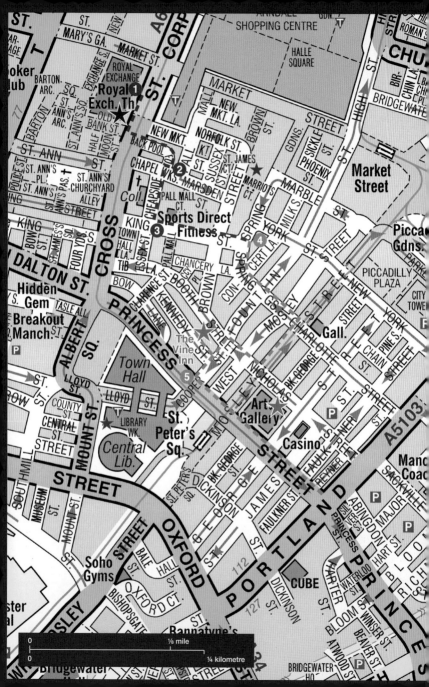

❶ Start at the Royal Exchange's Cross Street entrance. The various buildings of the Royal Exchange ★ were the centre of the global finished cotton industry for 200 years. This was when Manchester was 'Cottonopolis' and at one point controlled 80 per cent of the whole global trade. The main trading hall is one of the grandest commercial spaces in Europe and is worth a visit. It now hosts a startling theatre in the 'hi-tech' style of 1976. With your back to the entrance, turn right, following Cross Street. On the left-hand side of the road is a blue plaque. This marks the former offices of *The Manchester Guardian,* founded 1821, now *The Guardian* newspaper. Continue down the road and turn left into a tiny alleyway (a 'ginnel' to the locals) named Back Pool Fold. The pool it refers to surrounded Radcliffe Hall and was where 'lewds and scolds' – prostitutes and women who cheated with weights and measures – were ducked in water as a punishment.

❷ The ginnel surfaces at Sam's Chop House on Chapel Walks. 'Matchstick men' artist L. S. Lowry used to dine here and there's a life-size statue of him inside. Turn right, then immediately left along Cheapside. The modern office block on the right hosts a Unitarian church. The former building was where William Gaskell preached, the husband of renowned novelist Elizabeth Gaskell. At the junction with King Street, the building on the right is the former Lloyds Bank. This site was home to pioneering Doctor Charles White and later the site of the first Manchester Town Hall. A plaque on the wall commemorates a visit by a Japanese delegation that was instrumental in the Japanese industrial revolution.

❸ Turn left up King Street. The sandstone building with columns on the right is by Charles Cockerell and was the first permanent provincial Bank of England from 1846. The very large white Portland stone building next up on the right has Neptune at the roofline. This was the headquarters of Manchester Ship Canal (see Walk 16). Walk to the very top of the street and pause at the tall white Portland stone building, hosting Hotel Gotham. This is a masterpiece from 1935 by the architect of New Delhi's government buildings, Edwin Lutyens. The neo-Gothic building across King Street was the Reform Club, for the Liberal Party. At various times, Prime Ministers William Gladstone and Manchester-born David Lloyd George were hosted in the club and also with Winston Churchill when he was a Manchester MP.

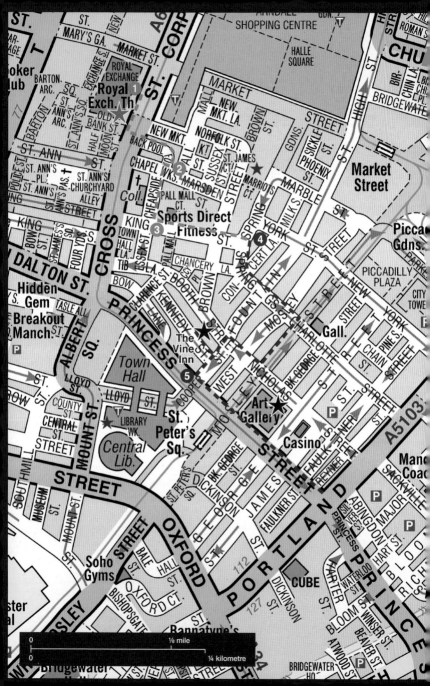

4 From the top of King Street follow Spring Gardens right to Mosley Street. Over the tramlines is the elegant portico of the aptly named Portico Library which you will encounter again on walk 2. Turn right on Mosley Street. Take the first right into Booth Street and turn left on Cooper Street. Stop outside the three pubs sitting all in a row and all from the late 18th century and early 19th century. The Vine Inn ★ , on Kennedy Street, has a top floor of continuous windows to let in light to aid the domestic system of textile production before it was overtaken by the arrival of full industrial production. This is a typical handloom weaver's cottage. The City Arms has great local beers. The Waterhouse pub here is named after the architect of Manchester Town Hall, who was a teetotal Quaker.

5 Turn left from Cooper Street into Princess Street and cross the tramlines. The neo-Greek Manchester Art Gallery ★ is on your left. This was completed in 1835, designed by the architect, Charles Barry, of the Palace of Westminster (Houses of Parliament) fame. Also by Charles Barry, and now part of the Gallery, is the next building on Princess Street, the former Athenaeum club. Barry set a precedent here, adapting an Italian Renaissance-style palace into a gentleman's club. Cotton manufacturers thought the model perfect for their warehouse/ showrooms in Manchester. Down the street, beyond the Athenaeum, all the bigger buildings were once textile warehouses and were called Manchester 'palazzos' after The Athenaeum. The walk concludes at the junction with Portland Street.

A̶Z walk three

Spinningfields

The modern city area with a deprived past.

John Rylands Library is one of the great research libraries of the UK. This is where you start a journey of Mancunian discovery through what is now a very new part of the city with a whole range of large offices and stylish food and drink venues but was once a byword for deprivation.

The tour takes you down to the River Irwell past a startling new courts building and a powerful museum which reminds us of the value of democracy. You will briefly cross into Manchester's twin city of Salford, learning the reason behind the name for the unit of energy. Back on the Manchester side of the river you find the origin of Manchester University, the first home of a famous soap opera and, in a lovely garden, a memorial to a man who, it is said, invented the weekend. You will also find a pair cannons.

The return is by one of the longest facades in the UK, a striking Art Deco building and a statue of a famous composer. This is an entertaining walk around a well-looked-after part of the city that was forgotten for many years but has latterly become a keystone in the Manchester experience.

start / finish	John Rylands Library, Deansgate
nearest postcode	M3 3EH
distance	1¼ miles / 2 km
time	1 hour
terrain	Paved roads and walkways.

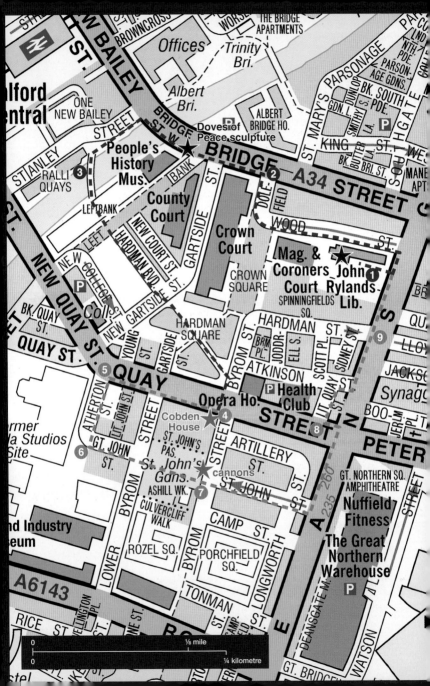

1 Start at John Rylands Library ★ at 150 Deansgate, built in 1899. This was one of the last great flowerings of Victorian Gothic architecture, with a grand and moody interior. It was gifted to the city by Enriqueta Rylands, widow of John Rylands, and designed by Basil Champneys. The building contains one of the top ten collections of manuscripts and printed material anywhere including a first folio of Shakespeare's plays, Guttenberg bibles, Newton's *Principia* and even oddities such as the 'Wicked Bible' from 1631. (This is so called because in the Ten Commandments the printer omitted the word 'not' in the seventh commandment: it reads 'Thou Shalt Commit Adultery'.) With your back to the library, turn left on Deansgate and take the first left, following the side of the library, down Wood Street. On the facade of 26 Wood Street you can read the words 'Street Mission'. This area of the city centre, Spinningfields, is filled with sharp modern structures and fashionable bars and restaurants but it was the 13th District in the mid-19th century, famous for its drunkenness, prostitution and poverty. Wood Street Mission was set up in 1869 by Alfred Alsop to help alleviate the condition of poverty-stricken children and their families. It continues its work today. Continue round the corner into Dolefield.

2 Turn left on Bridge Street and walk along to the large *Doves of Peace* sculpture ★ by Michael Lyons, which dates from 1986 and sits outside the People's History Museum. This museum charts the growth of democracy in the UK and is free to visit. The older part of the building incorporates one of the former pumphouses of central Manchester which provided hydraulic power to compress cotton bales, power industry and even turn the hands of the Town Hall clock. The huge Civil Justice Centre (2007) dominates everything in this part of the city with its 'filing cabinet' on the north and south elevations and its huge western glass wall. Designed by Denton Corker Marshall architects and containing 47 courts, it stands 266 feet (81 metres) tall. Cross over the River Irwell into Salford and turn left to the footbridge.

3 From the centre of the footbridge look back to the bridge you've just crossed. The tall building on the Salford side of the river at the bridge stands on the site of Benjamin Joule's brewery. His son James (1819–89) was a physicist who, partially inspired by observing the processes of brewing, developed his First Law of Thermodynamics. The unit of energy, the 'joule', is named after him. Continue over the footbridge, straight up Hardman Boulevard and on through the modern buildings of Spinningfields and across Hardman Square with its pleasant landscaping. Turn right at the tallest building, 1 Spinningfields, along Byrom Street, then right again onto Quay Street. Cross Quay Street at the pedestrian crossing.

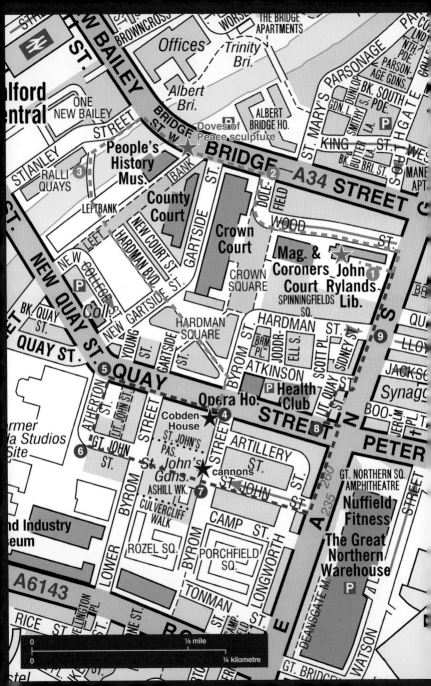

4 The large old residence here was home to Richard Cobden ★, political radical and exponent of the Manchester School of free trade. It was subsequently the first home of Owens College, from 1851, which became the present University of Manchester. Diagonally across the road is the Opera House from 1912 with its striking relief picked out in gold called *The Dawn of the Heroic Age*. Continue down the slope of Quay Street and turn left onto Atherton Street.

5 The building on the right is the former Granada Television headquarters. The studio here was once the home of *Coronation Street*. Granada was a pioneering commercial television channel founded in 1954 by Sidney Bernstein, who described the north as 'a closely knit, indigenous, industrial society; a homogeneous cultural group with a good record for music, theatre, literature and newspapers, not found elsewhere in this island.'

6 Turn left at Great John Street. The building on the corner was a former primary school. The terraced housing used to be so dense around here, the playground was on the flat roof. Cross Lower Byrom Street into St John's Gardens, the former cemetery of demolished St John's Church. The only remaining tomb on view is that of John Owens, who provided the money to create Owens College. William Marsden is also buried here. He 'invented the weekend' when he persuaded employers in the 1840s to allow workers

a half-day holiday on Saturdays. St John's Passage, on the north side of the gardens, sports two inverted Grade II listed cannons ★ now operating as bollards. They were placed here to mark the area where Bonnie Prince Charlie trained with his artillery during the abortive rebellion of 1745.

7 Leave the park from the opposite entrance you entered and continue straight ahead down St John Street, the best surviving street of Georgian townhouses in the city. Turn left onto Deansgate. Across the road is the long 'streaky bacon' facade of the Great Northern Goods Warehouse from the 1890s. Turn left onto Quay Street and then right onto Little Quay Street.

8 The vast white Portland stone building here is Sunlight House, designed by Joseph Sunlight. The building is an Art Deco behemoth from 1932 and anticipated modern co-working offices with lots of amenities including a swimming pool for office workers. Turn right on Atkinson Street and left along Deansgate and continue to the junction with Hardman Street.

9 Over the road and to the right is Queen Anne-style Elliot House from 1878 with lovely cherub lunette windows revealing its earlier existence as home of the city's School Board. Further along, across Deansgate, is a statue of Frederick Chopin who performed in Manchester. Continue down Deansgate the short distance to return to the start point.

A-Z walk four

The Ever-Changing City

Chinatown and Piccadilly.

Although the grid of streets in the city centre was laid out over two centuries ago, the buildings and their uses have continually changed over time to reflect the city's needs. The area explored on this circular walk formerly contained large Georgian town houses for Manchester's early 19th-century wealthy. Manchester Art Gallery (see walk 2) and the Portico Library have survived to represent the institutions they built themselves.

Money always talks though. All the houses disappeared as the wealthy left the centre for the suburbs, exploiting the commercial potential of the area and selling their properties off to become textile warehouses. As the textile trade declined, Cantonese businesses in Liverpool's Chinatown saw an opportunity and moved in during the 1980s and 1990s to create the largest Chinatown outside the capital. This is a proper 'village in a city' with food, shops, accountants, solicitors and casinos. In recent years the area has taken on a more Mandarin character but also Japanese, Thai and Vietnamese food outlets.

The route takes in the Piccadilly Gardens area, a place of permanent debate in Manchester. Every time it is redeveloped it never satisfies the locals. Along the way you will pass perhaps the single most sinister building in the region, as well as huge Brutalist buildings, ornate warehouses, a location where a famous UK institution was born and an unusual tree.

start / finish	Chinatown Arch, Faulkner Street
nearest postcode	M1 4FE
distance	1¼ miles / 2 km
time	1 hour
terrain	Paved roads and paths.

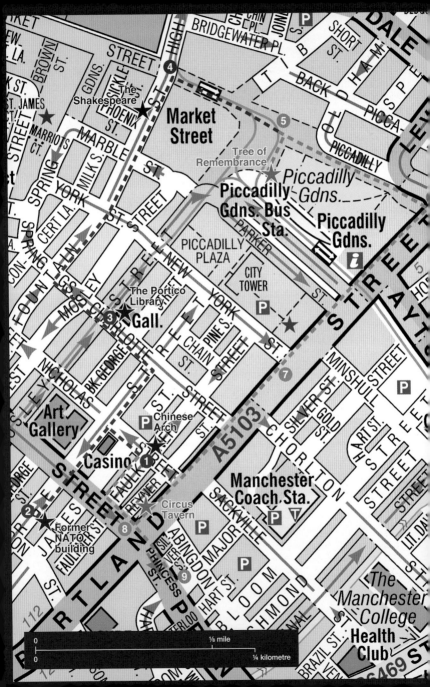

1 Start under the Chinese Arch ★ at Faulkner Street. This was a gift from China to Manchester in 1987 and is covered in reds, golds, greens and dragons and phoenixes, all symbolic of good fortune and happiness. Follow Nicholas Street, with the Chinese pavilion on your right, to George Street and turn left. Crossing Princess Street, continue on George Street, and stop at Manchester's most sinister building ★, surrounded by a razor wire-topped wall. This was built in the late 1950s as part of an underground NATO communications system in the event of a limited Soviet atomic attack. British Telecom now use it as part of their network.

2 Retrace your steps back across Princess Street into Chinatown and continue on George Street until you reach the junction with Charlotte Street. Turn left on Charlotte Street. On the right at the junction with Mosley Street is the Portico Library ★ from 1806 by Thomas Harrison, its name coming from the design of the facade on Mosley Street. You access this Age of Enlightenment building from the side door on Charlotte Street, ascending the stairs to a beautiful library space. Peter Mark Roget (of *Roget's Thesaurus* fame) was the first secretary. William Gaskell, husband of novelist Elizabeth Gaskell, was the second. Check out some of the famous visitors and members on the blue plaque outside.

3 Cross Mosley Street then take the second on the right, Fountain Street. Continue along Fountain Street for about 300 yards (275 metres), to the junction with Market Street, passing the black and white Shakespeare pub ★ on the left. This was originally constructed in Chester in the early 1600s but many of the details were moved to Manchester in the early 20th century. Under the first-floor eaves are entertaining 17th-century carvings – odd for a pub – of the dangers of drink including fighting, falling over, standing on your head and even riding a greased pig.

4 Turn right on Market Street. The first building on your right was once home of the mighty Lewis's department store. The next building along, at the corner where the trams turn, is a bank which sits on the site of the Royal Hotel. Plaques proclaim how the world's first football league was formally created in the hotel in April 1888, which explains why Manchester hosts the National Football Museum.

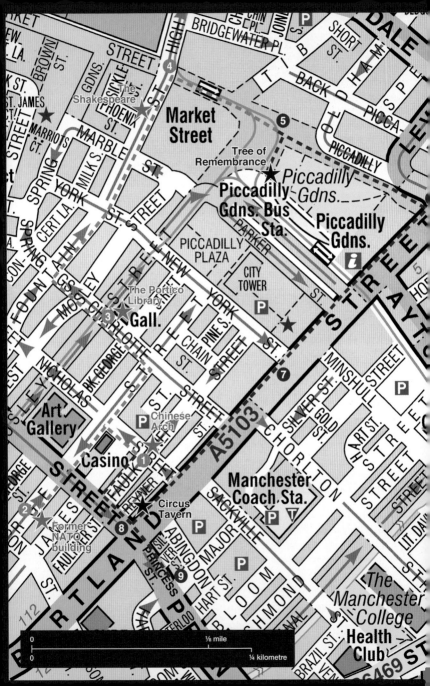

5 Turn right just before Piccadilly Gardens and walk along the line of trees that edge the grass. The last 'tree' is a metal sculpture: *The Tree of Remembrance* ★ , dedicated in 2005 to the Manchester civilians who lost their lives during the Second World War. Return to Market Street and continue with the gardens on your right. You will pass (unless masked by markets) the 19th-century statues of Sir Robert Peel and James Watt. The statue of Queen Victoria, unveiled in 1901, is by Edward Onslow Ford and was described as 'the most pretentious, incoherent, and inept sculptural monument in England'. Judge for yourself. While at the monument, take a look at the side of the 351-foot (107-metre) City Tower across the lawns of Piccadilly Gardens. With remarkable foresight for 1965, the designers decorated the length of the northeastern and southwestern elevations with stylized computer and radio circuitry.

6 After the Duke of Wellington statue, turn right down Portland Street and cross the tramlines. The vast Sixties complex in the Brutalist style of architecture here includes the oddly configured Mercure Hotel. There was a plan at the time for pedestrians to be separated from vehicles, the latter to navigate the city on elevated 'streets', hence the reception of the hotel is at car park level, high above street level. The hotel is always open so take the lift to reception but turn left out of the lift to the stairwell, where an abstract artwork by William Mitchell stretches through several floors.

7 Across the road is the Britannia Hotel. This building was the largest of the first generation of textile warehouses and opened in 1856 for the S&J Watts company. It was one of the few older buildings round here to survive the Second World War Blitz. The extravagant facade is matched by the extravagant main staircase in reception. The First World War Charles Sargeant Jagger war memorial to the left in the open entrance, *The Manchester Sentry*, is one of the most moving such memorials in the country. Continue down Portland Street, away from Piccadilly Gardens, to the junction with Princess Street. All the small properties on the right just before the junction survived because they were pubs serving the warehouse district. The Circus Tavern ★ claims to have the smallest bar area in the UK; it can only fit one person behind it.

8 Turn left down Princess Street to the junction with Major Street. The building on the other side of Major Street might look similar to all the other former textile warehouses in this area but this one was different. Designed by John Gregan in 1854, it was Manchester's second Mechanics Institute. In 1868 the Trades Union Congress (TUC) was formed here.

9 Turn round and follow Princess Street back across the junction with Portland Street, then take the second right to Faulkner Street to return to the Chinese Arch.

AZ walk five

The Ancient Heart of Two Cities

The old centres of Manchester and Salford.

When the Romans left in the fourth or fifth centuries AD, Manchester seems to have been completely deserted. Several decades later, or maybe as much as a century and a half later, the Anglo-Saxons arrived and settled here, in a very different part of the city to the Romans (see also walk 7).

In this location the Anglo-Saxons found it easier to protect themselves, above the cliffs on the Rivers Irwell and Irk, with a ditch cut between the two watercourses. The way the two modern cities have developed has done much to mask that geography, but it was from this fertile ground that modern Manchester and Salford would spring.

Here was the heart of what historian Asa Briggs called 'the shock city of age' as Manchester ballooned in size and significance and gloried in its self-styled epithet, 'What Manchester does today, London does tomorrow, and the world the day after'.

This circular walk covers the past, present and future of Manchester and Salford, underlining how the only constant of the two cities is change. There are grand buildings and humble buildings and rich stories.

start / finish	The National Football Museum, Cathedral Gardens
nearest postcode	M4 3BG
distance	1½ miles / 2.6 km
time	1 hour 15 minutes
terrain	Paved roads, some steps.

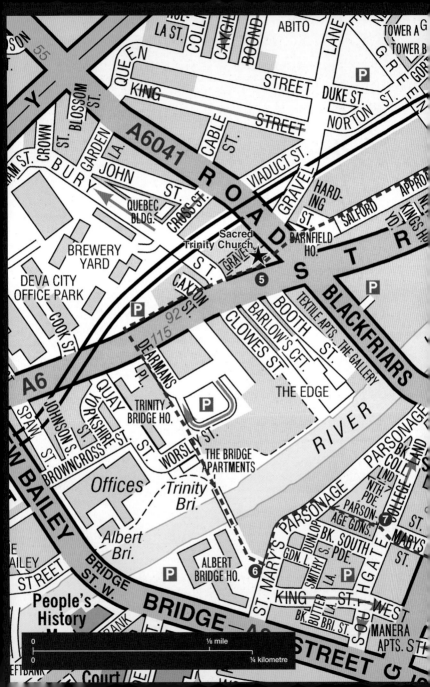

GATE

Salford
Bri.

P

HUNTS BANK

WALKER'S CFT.

VICTORIA STATION APP.

Lib.

Chetham's
Sch. of
Music

LONG MILLGATE

TODD ST.

LONG

P

P

MILLGATE

STREET

HANOVER

Robert
Owen statue

BALLOON ST.

CABLE ST.

IRA JON ST.

CATHEDRAL APP.

P

4

VICTORIA STREET

Glade
of Light

FENNEL

National
Football
Mus.

12

Odeon
Cinema

THE PRINTWORKS

GREENGATE
SQ.

E T

VICTORIA BRIDGE ST.

Cath.

3

CATH. YD.

CATH. GATES

HYDE'S CROSS

STREET

11 THE CORN
EXCHANGE

HANGING DITCH

PUMP
YD.

MARK.
LA.

BALLOON
LA.

Virgin Active

GDN. ST.

WELL
GRO.

DANTZIC ST.

LEVE ST.

SHUD

Vis. Cen.

CATEATON

EXCHANGE SQ.

ST.

NEW CATHEDRAL ST.

A56

E

Exchange
Sq.

T

T

EXCHANGE
COURT

T

WINTER
GDN.

T

A6042

CORPORATION

10

ARNDALE
SHOPPING CENTRE

ST.

MARY'S GA.

MARKET ST.

ROYAL
EXCHANGE

Royal
Exch. Th.

EXCHANGE ST.

9

ST.

HALLE
SQUARE

MARKET

T

MALL

NEW.
MKT.
LA.

BROWN ST.

STREET

GDNS.

SICKLE ST.

BARTON
ARC.

ANN'S SQ.

OLD
BANK ST.

ST. ANN'S ST.

HALF MOON ST.

NEW MKT.

BACK POOL
FO

NORFOLK ST.

KT.
ST.

SUSSEX
ST.

ST. JAMES
CT.

PHOENIX ST.

MARBLE

ANN

8

ST. ANN'S
PL.

ST. ANN'S
ARC.

T. ANN'S
PL.

ANN'S

ST.

ST. ANN'S PASS

ST. ANN'S
CHURCHYARD

ALLEY

STREET

CHAPEL WKS.

Coll.

CHEAPSIDE

PALL MALL
CT.

MARSDEN

PALL MALL ST.

MARRIOTS
CT.

SPRING

YORK

MILK ST.

ST.

Sports Direct
Fitness

① Start at the main entrance of The National Football Museum ★. In the pavement here is the Walk of Fame featuring famous male and female footballers. The world's first professional league was ratified in Manchester in April 1888 although neither Manchester United nor Manchester City were members. With your back to the museum entrance, turn right and follow the building wall down to Long Millgate and the water feature. Turn left on Long Millgate to Chetham's School of Music and Library. These were priest's quarters from 1421 before conversion to school and library in 1653. Daniel Defoe, Benjamin Franklin, Charles Dickens, Friedrich Engels and Karl Marx have all studied in the library, which is the oldest free public library in the English-speaking world.

② Facing Chetham's entrance, continue left up Long Millgate in the direction of Manchester Cathedral. Turn right down Fennel Street to the circular and sensitively conceived *Glade of Light* memorial ★ to the victims of the May 2017 attack on Manchester in which 22 people died. The Duke and Duchess of Cambridge (now the Prince and Princess of Wales) unveiled the memorial in May 2022. Turn left to the Cathedral.

③ Manchester Cathedral is not large because Manchester was a smallish market town before the Industrial Revolution. Do not be fooled by the building's size as it packs a punch

with sensational medieval woodwork, particularly in the choir. The nave ceiling sports a medieval orchestra of angels. The Cathedral was hit in 1940 by a bomb and among all the destruction the windows were blown out. New stained glass by Margaret Traherne and Antony Hollaway is another treasure. Thomas Clarkson, the abolitionist, gave a sermon in the Cathedral in 1787 which led to Manchester sending the first petition to Parliament demanding the end of the slave trade in the British Empire. To the right of the Cathedral is a recent statue of Mahatma Gandhi, a gift from the owners of Boohoo.com which is headquartered in the city. Behind is Hanging Ditch, a former stream, spanned by a medieval bridge. Turn your back on the Cathedral and walk towards the twin office buildings, prominently tagged 100 and 101 Embankment, crossing over the River Irwell, a tributary of the River Mersey.

④ Once over the river you are in Manchester's twin city of Salford. The surprisingly wide bridge, with the cobbled roadway here, was the approach to the long-gone Exchange Station which was linked to nearby Victoria Station. Together the linked stations had the longest platform in the world. Turn and look back towards the Cathedral sitting above the river. This is where Manchester began again after the Romans left. To the left of the Cathedral are the old 15th-century buildings in the pinky-red sandstone of Chetham's School of Music and

Library. That had been the location of an Anglo-Saxon fortification when they first arrived in the 6th or 7th century. This was a good defensive location perched on cliffs over the confluence of the Rivers Irk and Irwell. The modern city of Manchester developed from this location. Walk towards the office called 101 Embankment. On the left there is a covered structure with stairs leading to a car park that brings you out on Greengate. Cross Greengate straight through the new pedestrianized square of Embankment West, walking straight on to Blackfriars Street. Cross over to the Sacred Trinity Church ★ .

5 This attractive church, whose tower dates from the 1600s, contains one of the most moving of First World War memorials. There are 353 names of 'the officers, non-commissioned officers and men of the Salford Battalions of the Lancashire Fusiliers who fell … on July 1st 1916'. Follow the side of the church along Chapel Street. Turn left down Dearmans Place and re-cross the river into Manchester over the strikingly modern Trinity footbridge, close to the Lowry Hotel.

6 Turn left on St Mary's Parsonage and then, after a short distance, turn right on the path skirting Parsonage Gardens. This was the churchyard of St Mary's Church. As the city centre became a central business district many churches were demolished to make way for squares or gardens.

7 Continue down St Mary's Street and cross Deansgate to St Ann Street and elegant St Ann's Church ★ . This was consecrated in 1712. The top of the tower was traditionally where mapmakers triangulated distances as denoted by the benchmark arrow on its western side. If you see a sign saying, for example, 'Manchester 20 miles', it is to this point. The prime motivator for the church was Lady Ann Bland, who commemorated herself in the saint's name she chose for her church. She is Manchester's first recorded collector of art and introduced 'the harmonizing assembly'. She loved to wear the latest fashions, importing a doll from Paris decked in styles she could copy.

8 Turn left at the church, through St Ann's Square, passing the statue of Richard Cobden. Cobden engineered the Charter of Incorporation which gave the city its first modern council, he supported a national system of secular education and was a peace campaigner. He is best known for his association with fellow free trade campaigner John Bright. Famous words of Cobden include: 'At all events, arbitration is more rational, just and humane than resort to the sword' and 'For every credibility gap, there is a gullibility gap'. When he died, his great friend John Bright called him 'the manliest and gentlest spirit that ever quit or tenanted a human form'. Continue through the square to Market Street and turn right, with the Royal Exchange on your right.

9 Turn left on Corporation Street, passing a red post box with a plaque. This survived the IRA bomb attack of 1996 which led to this part of the city centre being rebuilt.

10 At Exchange Square, turn left and you arrive at two old pubs which were repositioned after the IRA bomb. The Old Wellington occupies a building from the 1530s and Sinclair's Oyster Bar dates from the 1730s. Lady Sarah Spittlewick used to devour huge numbers of oysters here in the 19th century but eventually swallowed one too many and choked on a pearl. She became an example to Mancunians of 'moderation in everything'. Descend the stairs at the pubs and take Cathedral Street to the right of Sinclair's Oyster Bar. The Cathedral is on the left and the handsome 1903 stone structure of the Corn Exchange on the right.

11 Turn right on Fennel Street. Follow the wall of the Corn Exchange, then cross Corporation Street and turn left with the National Football Museum on your left and the Printworks Entertainment complex on the right. At the junction with Balloon Street is a fine statue of Robert Owen, who lived in Manchester as he developed his co-operative theories which in turn inspired the Rochdale Pioneers in 1844. This first successful co-operative survives as the Co-operative Group, based in Manchester. Robert Owen would leave Manchester to set up New Lanark Mills in Scotland, now a World Heritage Site. The Co-operative Wholesale Society's former building at Balloon Street features shields high on the walls with names of international and UK cities in which it had a presence.

12 Retrace your steps on Corporation Street and turn right onto the left-hand pavement of Todd Street. Todd Street tracks part of the route of the former Toad Lane where Ann Lee was born. She became the leader of a Christian sect that became known as the Shakers, and portrayed herself as the female incarnation of Christ. Ann and her followers emigrated to America in 1774. A small community of Shakers lives on in Maine. The simple nature of their furniture was much admired by people such as Sir Terence Conran of the Habitat stores. Follow the glass wall of the National Football Museum back to your start point.

AZ walk six

Epic Architecture

Theatres, pubs and warehouses south of the
city centre.

Manchester's old theatre district was once all along Oxford Street; that's not
quite the case today but there are still plenty of live entertainment venues
to see on this walk. The area you walk through has also been an industrial
and commercial powerhouse with a very varied streetscape and a legacy of
fascinating architecture.

The circular walk starts at The Bridgewater Hall then follows a typical city
centre route that takes in water as well as paving, following a canal towpath
to the theatres and cinemas of the HOME arts centre. In front of this is a
statue of a German gentleman who lived in Manchester for years and whose
experience here had a profound historical effect. From there you encounter
old factories converted into new uses, including one which gave a name to a
famous garment and another which is home to the archive of a well-known
and proud Mancunian writer.

One of the greatest monuments of Manchester's commercial prowess is
the magnificent former Refuge Assurance Company, a phantasmagoria in
terracotta which sports busy bees on its landmark clock tower. The return
takes in more contrasts, with huge warehouses and humble but handsome
pubs, and ends with an award-winning monument to the city's low-carbon
commitment. This is a walk with drama both in its history and its architecture.

start / finish	The Bridgewater Hall, Lower Mosley Street
nearest postcode	M2 3WS
distance	1¼ miles / 2 km
time	1 hour 15 minutes
terrain	Paved roads and paths. Boardwalk and steps.

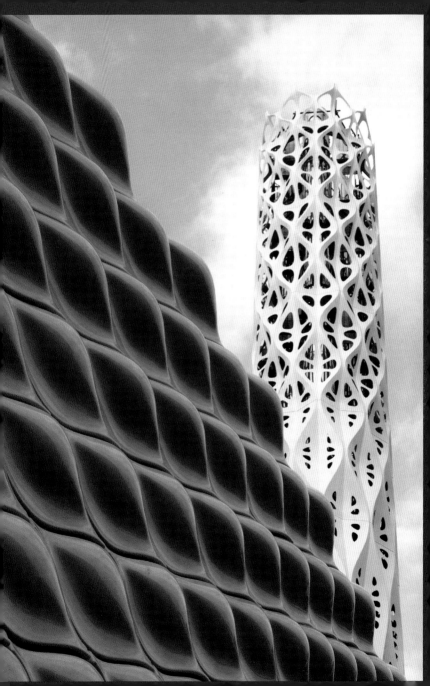

❶ Start at The Bridgewater Hall ★ in Barbirolli Square off Lower Mosley Street. The hall, opened in 1996, is the 2,355-capacity concert hall for classical music in the city and the principal home of the Hallé orchestra. Note the black rubber seal in front of the main entrance. This marks the division between Mother Earth and the auditorium. All 22,500 tons of the latter sit on a bed of 280 springs to shield it from external noise. With your back to the main entrance, turn right down the stairs and follow the boardwalk by the pretty canal basin with its fountain, to the junction with the Rochdale Canal. Turn right along the Rochdale Canal past Lock 89 and then cross the footbridge and turn left. The canal was vital to the development of much of south-central Manchester and the towns to the east. When it was completed, in 1804, goods could be transhipped right across the north of England from the Irish Sea on the west coast to the North Sea on the east.

❷ Turn immediately right at the far end of the lock and descend the slope to Whitworth Street West. Cross over to Jack Rosenthal Street, under the arch, named after the Manchester playwright. Follow Jack Rosenthal Street to Tony Wilson Place, named for the Manchester music and broadcasting impresario. The large statue ★ here is of the German communist and Manchester businessman Friedrich Engels who lived for 22 years in Manchester, on and off, from 1842. As part of a controversial art project, the statue was recovered from Ukraine in 2017. The adjacent black building is HOME, with its five arthouse cinemas, two theatres and an art gallery.

❸ Retrace your steps a few yards/ metres and turn right down the other branch of Jack Rosenthal Way to James Grigor Square. Turn immediately left and then right into Wilmott Street and then left onto Hulme Street. The former mill on the left here is Macintosh Mills (1825–6) ★, famous for the production of the eponymous raincoat. Cross Cambridge Street but keep on Hulme Street, passing the International Anthony Burgess Foundation with its study and event centre together with the archive of the famous Manchester author of *A Clockwork Orange*.

❹ Turn left onto Great Marlborough Street, straight under the railway bridge to The Ritz ★ on Whitworth Street West. The Ritz is one of Manchester's oldest music halls, dating from 1928 and where cult Manchester band The Smiths first performed in 1982. Turn right at the Ritz towards Oxford Street.

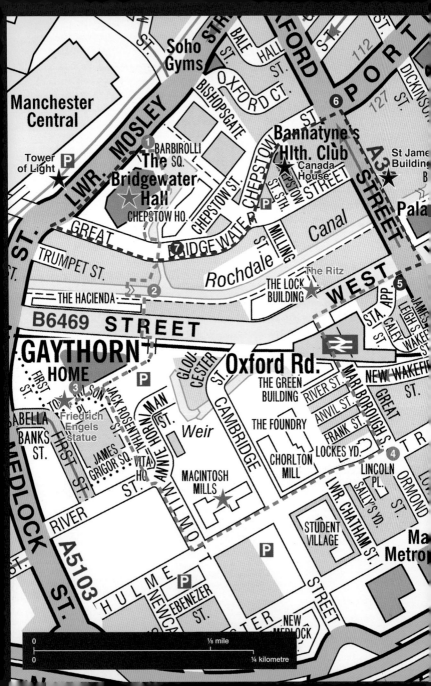

5 At the traffic lights, cross over Oxford Street and study the vast bulk of the former Refuge Assurance Company headquarters, now the Kimpton Clocktower Hotel. There is so much symbolism on this building designed by Alfred Waterhouse and, later, his son Paul. The 1903 corner entrance supports a castle gatehouse hinting that your money is safe with the Refuge; the 1910 tower sports a large clock with one of the city symbols, the Manchester bee, spreading its wings at 12, 3, 6 and 9 on the dial. If you have time, take a look inside the spectacular building. Cross over to the Palace Theatre, opened in 1891, plain on the outside, gorgeous on the inside, with a blue plaque to Manchester comedian Les Dawson. Continue up Oxford Street. The next building on the right, St James's Buildings ★, looks like a Baroque palace but is a former textile warehouse, built in 1913 in white Portland stone for the Calico Printers' Association. It is now general offices. There are other huge former textile warehouses on the other side of the street.

6 At the junction with Portland Street, cross Oxford Street and follow Chepstow Street, passing the fine textile warehouse of Canada House ★, built in 1909 by W. & G. Higginbottom, with its Art Nouveau gate. The whole rear of the building is glazed to allow in light. Chepstow Street becomes Great Bridgewater Street with, on the left, the delightful Peveril of the Peak pub with its Art Nouveau tiling. Inside, the pub is said to have the oldest continuously used table football machine, from the 1950s.

7 On the other side of the Pev (as it's known) is the lovely brick warehouse, now apartments, from 1874 called Chepstow House. Continuing down to the junction with Lower Mosley Street you come to The Britons Protection pub from the first years of the 19th century. This is another lovely pub with an original interior. Over the road is the award-winning Tower of Light ★, completed in 2022, which is part of the Civic Quarter Heat Network. The fantasy-like flue is from engineer architects Tonkin Liu while the rippling white tiles of the 'Wall of Energy' were made by Darwen Terracotta. Turn right up Lower Mosley Street to return to the start point.

AZ walk seven

Romans, Canals and Railways

Urban history and regeneration in Castlefield.

Castlefield is a remarkable part of the city centre. Here, water, iron, steel, brick and stone create a hard-edged but powerful man-made landscape that's been a favourite of disparate interest groups such as film crews and industrial archaeologists seeking the drama of the urban landscape.

It is an area of huge significance for the city and beyond. This is where the UK's pioneering artificial waterway meets the first canal to cross the Pennine hills, where the oldest passenger railway station anywhere sits inside one of the largest museums of Science and Industry. It is also where Manchester began. There is no evidence of permanent human settlement before AD 79 and the arrival of the Romans, who built a fort in this part of the future city.

Part of the intriguing nature of Castlefield is that while there might be reminders of the very oldest that Manchester has to offer, there are also the very newest. The city has pushed the development, just to the southeast of the area, of a huge cluster of very tall towers, between forty and sixty storeys tall. This contrast is, for many if not all, invigorating. Here again is mighty human engineering in an area that's defined by ambition in building impressive and practical landmarks.

start / finish	Science and Industry Museum, Lower Byrom Street
nearest postcode	M3 4FP
distance	1½ miles / 2.5 km
time	1 hours
terrain	Paved roads and paths. Steps.

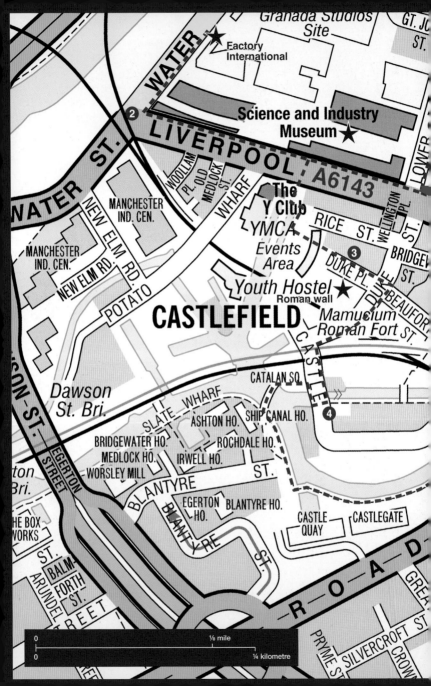

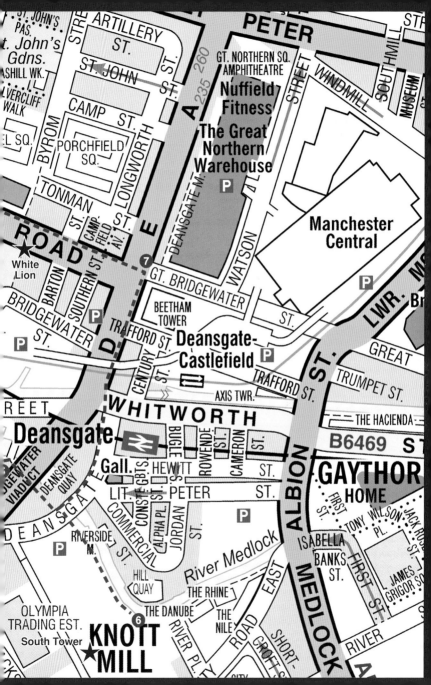

1 Start outside the main entrance of the Science and Industry Museum ★ on Lower Byrom Street. This occupies original 19th-century railway buildings and includes a rich collection of steam trains and engines, textile machines and much more. It's free, with the Revolution Manchester gallery providing real insight into the city and region's many 'firsts'. With your back to the entrance of the museum, turn right and then right again on Liverpool Road. As you turn, glance across the road at Oxnoble pub, perhaps the only UK pub named after a potato, sold in the former markets here. You pass a street called Potato Wharf on the way down Liverpool Road to the long range of sandstone buildings on the right. These Grade I listed buildings, now part of the Science and Industry Museum, were formerly Liverpool Road Station, the oldest passenger railway station in the world, with the oldest surviving railway warehouse. They were opened in 1830 by the Duke of Wellington as part of the Liverpool and Manchester Railway. The Commercial Hotel here can lay claim to being the first railway hotel in the world.

2 Turn right at the bottom of Liverpool Road into Water Street. After passing under a pair of railway viaducts, Water Street soon opens out into the public square which, from summer 2023, is in front of the 7,000-capacity Factory International ★ 'cultural space'. The splendid landscaping here includes references to the neighbouring infrastructure developments from 1761 involving water and rail. There's a grandstand view of George Stephenson's 1830 railway viaduct. Retrace your steps to Liverpool Road and walk back up the hill. First right after Potato Wharf, take the steps down the slope into Castlefield Bowl, an events arena. Cross in front of Castlefield Bowl, climbing the stairs in the middle of the stone seating area, up to the reconstructed Roman fort wall ★.

3 Manchester was founded by the Romans in AD 79 under General Agricola. It was an important location in the northwest of England between the legionary fortresses at Chester and York and a junction for a network of roads. At its heyday it had an 800-strong mixed garrison of infantry and cavalry. Early Christian worship is evidenced by a 'magic square', a coded inscription spelling 'Paternoster', found in the 1970s and dating from around AD 175–185. Part of the west wall and north gate of the fort, along with their attendant ditches, have been reconstructed. Manchester's Roman name is believed to be Mamucium, 'the breast-shaped hill'. Turn right on Duke Street and left beneath the mighty steel railway viaducts (1880s to 1890s) to Rochdale Canal, which you cross over on the cobbled road.

4 You are standing at the junction of Rochdale Canal from 1804 and the Bridgewater Canal from 1761, close to the very pretty lockkeeper's cottage. Nearby are former stables, warehouses and mills in brick, all given new uses.

Look back at the railway viaducts, whose construction wiped out most of the Roman fort site. The Victorians illustrated where they'd destroyed the fort by capping the viaduct piers with little castles. Retrace your steps back over the Rochdale Canal and turn left into Catalan Square. Cross the white curving bridge over the Bridgewater Canal and follow the towpath left, crossing one small bridge, all the way round to a footbridge with an old church behind.

5 You have been walking on the towpath of the Bridgewater Canal engineered by James Brindley and John Gilbert. This was the Britain's first canal of the industrial age and brought coal 7 miles (11 km) from Worsley (see walk 20) into Manchester; it was later extended to the Mersey Estuary. The vast profits made by the Duke of Bridgewater encouraged the rapid expansion of canals across the country, a period that became known as 'Canal Mania'. Across the canal here is a partially reconstructed Grocers' Warehouse which housed a waterwheel that lifted coal to road height. The former church seen here from 1858 once housed record producer Pete Waterman's studio. Do not cross the footbridge but continue straight on under the road bridge and the apartment block. Cross Deansgate into the Deansgate Square complex, with its tall towers, to walk by the landscaped riverside.

6 This cluster of tall residential towers is by far the tallest outside London, designed by Manchester-based SimpsonHaugh architects and well known for the clever way they catch the light. South Tower ★ is 659 feet (201 metres) tall. The river here is the River Medlock, which flows in a tunnel under the Bridgewater Canal basin from this point, thus excess canal water could be drained into the river and water dropped into the river could turn a wheel to lift goods to road level as at Grocers' Warehouse. Retrace your steps to Deansgate and turn right to the pedestrianized area under the railway viaduct. Cross Whitworth Street West and continue on Deansgate as far as Liverpool Road.

7 Turn left along Liverpool Road to the White Lion pub ★, a late 18th-century pub that sits adjacent to 'Roman Gardens', where several foundations of buildings of the small settlement that developed outside the Roman fort are exposed. Also on Liverpool Road are several weavers' cottages, with their long rows of workshop windows on the second floor to bring in light. Over the road is a rare blue post box which for a few years in the 1930s were for airmail only. Across the road is a former market hall from the 1870s, part of a markets complex here, now with other uses. Continue down Liverpool Road and turn right into Lower Byrom Street and the start point of this tour at the Science and Industry Museum.

AZ walk eight
The Northern Quarter

Kooky hospitality and street art.

This is boho Manchester, filled with indie shops and bars set amidst the strong bones of old market buildings and 'Cottonopolis' warehouses from its textile heyday.

Look out for the street and public art which adds interest to this circular walk. The street pattern is a grid running southwest to northeast and northwest to southeast. Streets on the former axis have their names in blue on white tiles and the latter have their names in white on blue tiles. This provides a good way of orientating yourself. Some of the artworks refer to this area being a former centre for the pet shop trade. All of the art underlines the Northern Quarter's character as a place for artists, graphic designers and other 'creatives'. The route takes you past a wacky bazaar that has often inspired that creativity.

Don't expect too much in the way of greenery or even much space; the streets are often narrow and the action comes thick and fast. The Northern Quarter of Manchester is an intensely urban environment which explains why it has been used in television and films as a very dynamic city backdrop, often doubling as North American cities.

start / finish	Stevenson Square
nearest postcode	M1 1LW
distance	1¼ miles / 2 km
time	1 hour
terrain	Paved roads and walkways.

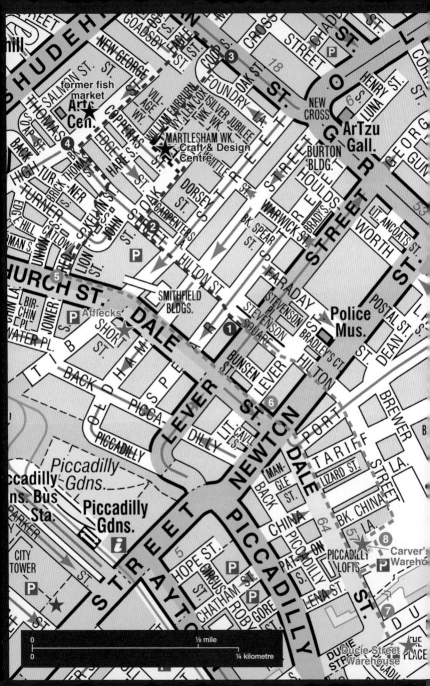

1 Begin outside the Fred Aldous shop on the southwest side of Stevenson Square. Art supplier Aldous is the second-oldest retailer in the city, from 1886. Stevenson Square, which developed after 1780, is filled with graffiti art and has always been a very democratic space, formerly serving as the Speaker's Corner for the city. The Mancunian leader of the Suffragettes, Emmeline Pankhurst, was one of many to create a platform for her opinions here. From Stevenson Square, with your back to the shop, turn left and follow Hilton Street, crossing Oldham Street, past the most notorious karaoke pub in Manchester, The Millstone, to Oak Street.

2 On the left is the ugly 1970s car park which has come in useful in TV productions such as *Life on Mars*, which was set in the 1970s. There's a curious sculpture of a dustpan and brush called *A New Broom* in front of the car park, by George Wylie. This represents the changes in the area since the 1990s. Turn right up Oak Street. Keep your eyes peeled between the buildings for murals covering two gable ends. Both are part of the Cities of Hope project highlighting the plight of excluded communities. The one on the right here shows Manchester writer Anthony Burgess, famous for his dystopian novel, *A Clockwork Orange*. A little further up the street is the Manchester Craft & Design Centre ★, occupying a former retail fish market (1873), it is now filled with charming retail outlets. Walk through the building if open, if not, follow Copperas Street along the side of the building. At the back of the Craft & Design Centre, turn right into the pedestrian pathway of William Fairbairn Way. Continue up the narrow Coop Street to Swan Street.

3 Turn left on Swan Street. The building immediately on the left here is Mackie Mayor, a former meat market from 1857, now a food hall with a splendidly airy interior. Walk through Mackie Mayor to the Eagle Street entrance and turn left. If closed, continue down Swan Street and take the first left into Eagle Street and continue straight on. Eagle Street becomes High Street with, on the right, the impressive facade of the former wholesale fish market ★. Try and spot, on the gable of a nearby building, a pineapple from 1994 by Kate Malone, a symbol of hospitality in an area now defined by hospitality.

4 Turn left into Thomas Street then take the second right down tiny Kelvin Street, past some restored weavers' cottages with their second-floor windows almost spanning the building. These rooms were workshops and brought light into the workspace with the family living below. You will emerge into Turner Street with, to the right, the Abel Heywood pub, named for one of the city's greatest mayors, a printer, publisher and radical. Turn left in front of the Abel Heywood and continue down Red Lion Street to Church Street.

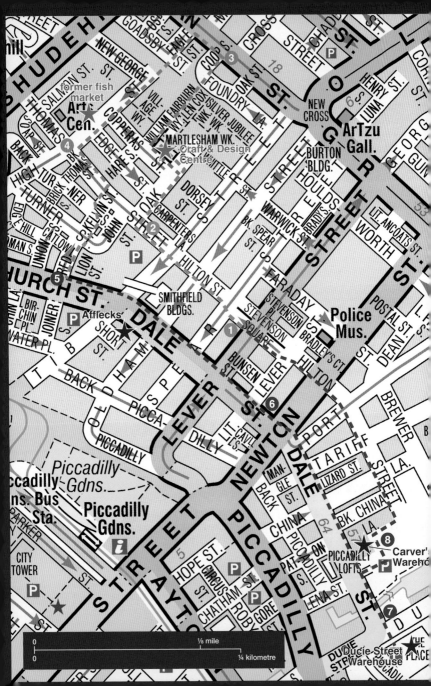

5 Turn left to the junction with Tib Street. Cross Church Street to look at the mosaic panels by Mark Kennedy on Afflecks ★, the maverick and fascinating bazaar that has been at the heart of Manchester's indie and alternative scene since 1982. It is worth a wander round. Featured on the mosaic panels are people and brands associated with the city such as Tony Wilson, Emmeline Pankhurst, George Best, Morrissey, Liam Gallagher, Friedrich Engels, *Coronation Street* characters, Rolls Royce, Vimto and many others. Continue on to Dale Street. All the large old buildings here are former textile warehouses.

6 In the block on the left after the junction with Lever Street is 25–27 Dale Street, a recent building replacing a warehouse lost to fire. By Falconer Chester Hall Architects, it is a lesson in how to build an unmistakably modern building respectful of context and location. Continue on Dale Street over Newton Street. You might have seen this stretch of Dale Street on TV and film. In the Marvel Avengers' movie *Captain America*, there was a chase scene in which Dale Street doubled as New York's Lower East Side in the 1940s. This part of Manchester has often doubled as New York or Chicago. The warehouse cityscape resembles areas in those cities, or rather they resemble Manchester.

7 At the end of Dale Street, the 1860s building facing you across Ducie Street is Ducie Street Warehouse ★, now a coffee shop, restaurant and aparthotel. It is always open, so enter and take a look at the scale of the main interior space. Return down Dale Street but turn right after the canal under the large arch into the surface car park. Turn left in front of the handsome stone building, Carver's Warehouse, from 1806. This has two large arches at ground level which reveal its original function. The area now occupied by the car park used to be a large canal basin where the Rochdale and Ashton Canals met, and boats would load and offload into Carver's Warehouse. Many of the canal arms and basins were infilled with rubble from bomb sites after the Second World War as it was thought canals would be redundant in the motor vehicle age.

8 After passing in front of Carver's Warehouse ★, turn right and then left onto Hilton Street. Follow Hilton Street all the way back to the start point in Stevenson Square.

ᴀᴢ walk nine

Park and Pride

The new Mayfield Park and Manchester's Gay Village.

If there is one complaint Mancunians have about their city centre, it is the lack of green space.

Mayfield Park might be on the fringe of the city in a huge area of redevelopment, but this park, opened in 2022, is both beautiful and clever. It makes good use of a river which has been culverted for decades and helps start to remedy the city centre's lack of greenery. As well as taking a spin through Mayfield, this walk also passes some of the huge terracotta buildings around the Whitworth Street area before taking a turn through Manchester's famous Gay Village, which is especially lively in the evenings and during high days and holidays.

The reason for the number of terracotta buildings in the city is due to Manchester's industrial-age chemical soup of an atmosphere turning stone buildings black with soot. Glazed tiles prevented soot penetrating the fabric of the buildings and thus made them almost self-cleaning. The detailing on these buildings is extravagant, symbolic of their previous functions, and is worth lingering over.

This circular walk also features a famous Manchester drink, the tragic story of a great scientist and the more upbeat story of a famous engineer who helped make all our lives easier.

start / finish	Manchester Piccadilly Railway Station, Fairfield Street entrance
nearest postcode	M1 2PN
distance	1¾ miles / 2.9 km
time	1 hour 15 minutes
terrain	Paved roads and paths.

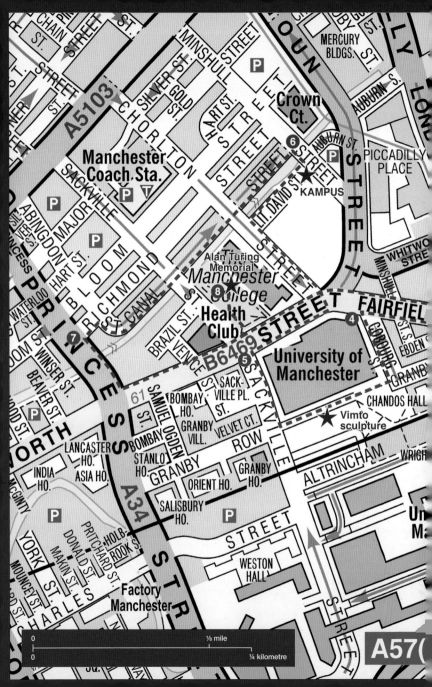

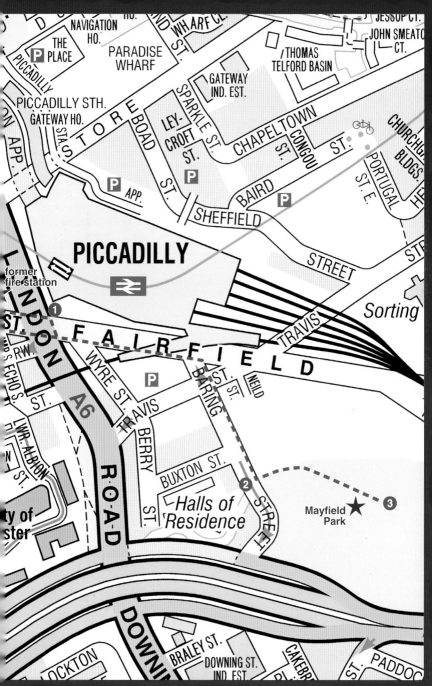

1 Start the tour close to the taxi rank of Piccadilly Station, at the junction of London Road and Fairfield Street. Cross Fairfield Street at the traffic lights and turn left, past the station and under the railway bridge. Turn right into Baring Street and follow it down the slope past the huge disused Mayfield Depot, now a fabulous and moody entertainment venue. On the left just before the River Medlock there is a large metal girder high overhead marking the entrance to Mayfield Park ★.

2 Turn into the 6.5-acre, £23 million park which opened on 22 September 2022 and take a spin around its fine landscape, designed by Studio Egret West. This area was poisoned by 200 years of industrialization, and the turnaround is remarkable. A main feature is the River Medlock, which for 150 years partially skulked under a culvert here. In the Great Flood of July 1872 a cemetery wall upstream of Mayfield was torn down by the waters and scores of bodies were released, swept along the river through the present park area. As the contemporary ballad goes: 'Ghastly forms of old and young / Lay open to our view / God grant that such appalling sights / May ne'er be seen by you!'.

3 Return along Baring Street and Fairfield Street, past the start point at Piccadilly Station. The huge buff-terracotta bulk of the former London Road Fire Station ★ across the road can't be missed. Now offices and apartments, it was created as a monument to civic pride in 1906 and included 38 flats for officers and families plus Manchester Coroner's Court. A walk around the building reveals lots of delightful details; look out for the fire spirits and the water nymphs and female personifications of Night and Day – a fire station works 24 hours after all. Cross London Road and walk down Fairfield Street, with the old fire station on your right.

4 Turn left on Cobourg Street and then right on Granby Row until you encounter an oversized bottle of Vimto ★ surrounded by its oversized ingredients. The popular drink was invented on this site in 1908 by J. N. Nichols. Follow Granby Row to Sackville Street and turn right. The huge building you are walking round is the former Technical School from 1902, again with lots of entertaining terracotta. On top of the building is the Godlee Observatory, named for the sponsor Francis Godlee in 1903. He was an early technological adopter; his phone number was 4.

5 Turn right onto Whitworth Street, back in the direction of the London Road Fire Station but turn left up Chorlton Street at the traffic lights. Just before the Rochdale Canal, swerve right down the cobbled Little David Street, between 19th-century warehouses and into the KAMPUS development ★ , with its fine new urban garden on the site of a filled-in canal arm. Leave by the entrance opposite to where you came in, turn left onto Minshull Street and then, across the canal, immediately left down the side of Rochdale Canal.

6 The large and elaborate neo-Gothic building on the right as you turn, now extended, is Crown Courts, designed by Thomas Worthington and opened in 1871. Follow the pedestrianized Canal Street for 350 yards (320 metres), over Chorlton Street and Sackville Street to Princess Street. This is the heart of the Gay Village and the centre of the Pride celebrations in August. The three old pubs here were known as 'queer' places in the 19th century, with homosexuality and prostitution semi-tolerated in an area where few people lived. It was the obvious place for the Village to develop in more recent times.

7 Turn left on Princess Street and then left on Whitworth Street. Cross Sackville Street and enter Sackville Gardens. There are several artworks here but, most prominently, a statue of Alan Turing ★ sat on a bench holding an apple. The scientific genius and polymath, famous for his work at Bletchley Park in cracking the Nazi Enigma code, was working at Manchester University when he was found guilty of homosexuality in 1952, then a criminal offence. This led to his suicide by poisoned apple – his favourite pantomime as a child had been Snow White.

8 Return to Whitworth Street and turn left. This street was named after Joseph Whitworth (1803–87). He was one of the city's greatest philanthropists and 'the father of precision engineering'. Perhaps his greatest invention was the standard screw gauge, which means today everybody uses the same screw gauge to change plugs and fix machines. Continue along Fairfield Street, which takes you back to the start point at Piccadilly Station.

A walk ten

Angels in the North

The Co-operative headquarters and other interesting sites.

This area of the city, in the northern part of the centre, is defined by infrastructure and the global Co-operative (Co-op) movement. You will start at Victoria Station and walk through the former office and workshops of the Co-op, now becoming empty as the company relocates all its head office functions to a new and very large building which you also pass.

Most of central Manchester is flat but here there is landscape variation as you walk on the eastern slopes of the River Irk and pass a curious pub with a spectacular interior and a floor which bizarrely follows the contours of the hill.

There is some bold 1960s architecture, once derided and now admired, some fine new landscaping and a pleasant small park surrounded by old and new buildings. As always in the city, you will find reminders of former industry and commerce mixed in with new apartments and offices. In the midst of life there is also death, and that pleasant park you pass through hides a sombre secret. Perversely, it also holds a much more entertaining revelation as well.

The return journey reveals how street names often contain a rich history of their own. This circular walk takes in an area of Manchester that is set to continue developing at a fast pace.

start / finish	Manchester Victoria Station, main entrance on Victoria Station Approach
nearest postcode	M3 1WY
distance	1¼ miles / 1.9 km
time	1 hour
terrain	Paved roads and paths.

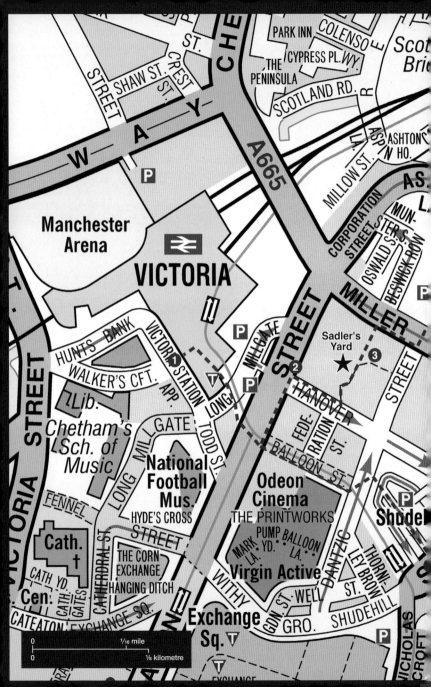

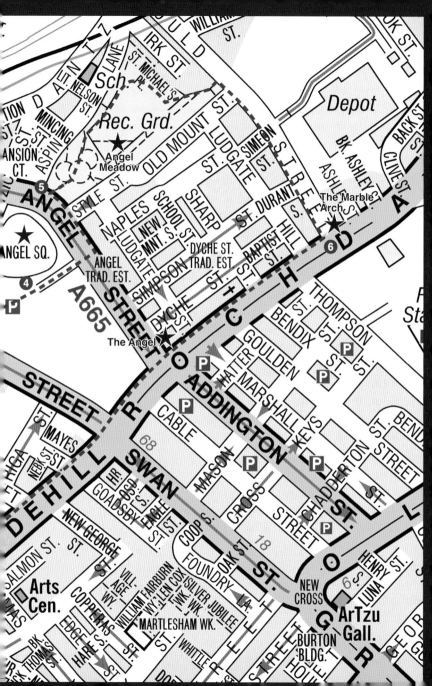

❶ Begin on the other side of the road from Victoria Station, facing the glazed canopy. The canopy features names of rail destinations across northern England but also in Belgium, as the station builders, the Lancashire and Yorkshire Railway, owned ferries to the Low Countries. This main facade is from 1909; the lower element to the left, at right angles to the main building, is George Stephenson's original station from 1844. Take a look inside the station at the flamboyant war memorial by George Wragge, a huge painted wall map and an Edwardian domed bar. Leave the station by the entrance adjacent to the tramlines (at the right-hand end of the station from where you entered). There is a people's memorial to the victims of the 2017 Arena attack here and the 'soldiers' gate' through which thousands of troops left during the First World War. It features, in plan, the main war cemeteries in France and Belgium. From the station entrance, follow the tramlines to Corporation Street and turn left.

❷ At Hanover Street, turn right and walk to the landscaped square of Sadler's Yard ★ on the left. All the buildings in this area were built by the Co-operative movement, the best older ones being the two Dutch modernist buildings in yellow brick by Johnson and Cropper. The building at the northern end of the square, New Century, is by Tait and Hay. It dates from 1963 in the International Modern style and is based on Mies van der Rohe's Crown Hall in Chicago. It now has a food hall on the ground floor and a state-of-the-art college for music and gaming in the basement. Upstairs is the sumptuous auditorium with a sprung dancefloor and gorgeous art by Stephen Sykes. Mothballed for years and now reopened, in the past it has hosted The Hollies, Jimi Hendrix, Tina Turner and famous Northern Soul nights.

❸ Take the tunnel-like exit from Sadler's Yard and turn right up Miller Street, crossing the road at the pedestrian crossing. You are now in Angel Square. The Grade II CIS Tower from 1962 lies back across the road and is being redeveloped as modern offices. At 25 storeys, 400 feet (122 metres), it was the tallest office block in Europe for a while. With the whole 1960s complex, the Co-op wanted the most up-to-date headquarters in Europe. The huge replacement Co-op headquarters, 1 Angel Square ★, is set in landscaped gardens and opened in 2012, designed by 3DReid. It was a pioneer in sustainable building. The three black funnels protruding from the ground are sculptural but also part of the ventilation system.

4 Walk past the right side of the new Co-op headquarters building on the higher ground. The development area on the right was the site of the very first steam-powered factory from Richard Arkwright in 1783. Having chosen to site the mill away from a river, Arkwright demonstrated his intention to use steam power rather than water power. As one account puts it: 'This technical shift signalled the birth of the steam-powered textile mill, and the beginning of the rise of Manchester as a factory metropolis'. The mill was destroyed by Second World War bombing. Cross Angel Street at the lights and turn left.

5 Turn right into Angel Meadow ★. This pleasant green space hides a secret. The upper area was the graveyard of long-gone St Michael's Church. Burials took place from 1789 to 1854. The lower area was a new parish burial ground in use from 1789 to 1815. Together, these relatively small areas hold more than forty thousand dead. Some of the memorial stones remain in the upper part of the graveyard. The lower part was once covered with flagstones and perversely renamed a 'recreation ground'. 1966 World Cup winner Nobby Stiles would kick a ball around here as a child. *Coronation Street* creator Tony Warren said the names of the original 1960 characters came from combining names together from the gravestones. Walk through Angel Meadow, taking the path round the left-hand side. Look across the road to the left to see the older red-brick building, formerly the Charter Street Ragged School. This was once a desperately poor area. The names of these charity schools pulled no punches as to the economic position of their pupils. Exit the park via the gate at the far end, then turn right into Gould Street.

6 The Marble Arch pub ★ is at the junction with Rochdale Road. If the pub is open, pop your head in for a glimpse of the stunning tile and mosaic interior from theatre designer Alfred Darbyshire, from the 1880s. The names of the drinks available are amusing, the sloping floor almost following the contours of the ground beneath is bemusing. Turn right down Rochdale Road passing The Angel pub ★, just along Angel Street to the right, a reminder of the late Georgian houses that occupied the area. Cross the major junction with Miller Street and continue straight down Shudehill until you reach the tramlines, passing some entertaining pub facades, masking 18th-century buildings, on The Hare and Hounds and The Lower Turk's Head.

7 Turn right through the tram station, following the tramlines to Balloon Street, which takes you back to Victoria Station. The street is named for pastry chef turned aviator James Sadler and his balloon ascents in 1785. The first ascent went smoothly, the second not so. Sadler was blown forty miles over the Pennines and had to pay compensation to a farmer. As it came down in a field, the balloon had killed a cow.

AZ walk eleven

Soaring Mills and Posh Restaurants

The districts of Ancoats and New Islington.

Nowhere in Manchester has the city changed as much as in the area explored on this walk. To the northeast of the city centre, the district of Ancoats was once a creature of smoky factories and terraced houses. It still contains traces of both, but the former workers would be amazed at the swish new apartments and the district's growing reputation as one of the most exciting food and drink destinations in the country.

One of the restaurants is called Elnecot, the original name of the area, which is old English for 'lonely cottage'. When factory owners and entrepreneurs learned at the end of the 18th century that the Rochdale Canal was about to traverse the area, they moved in quickly. Infrastructure meant an opportunity to tranship your products.

From fields and isolated houses, Ancoats changed almost overnight. People travelled from across Europe and the wider world to view an area christened 'the first industrial suburb'. 'Here are [factory] buildings seven to eight storeys, as high and as big as the Royal Palace in Berlin,' said the famous German architect Schinkel in 1825.

Along the way, you will also see inside a transformed mill and take a look at the newly created suburb of New Islington, while giving a nod to a famous artist associated with the city.

start / finish	Junction of Oldham Street & Great Ancoats Street
nearest postcode	M4 1LJ
distance	1¼ miles / 2 km
time	1 hour
terrain	Paved roads, steps.

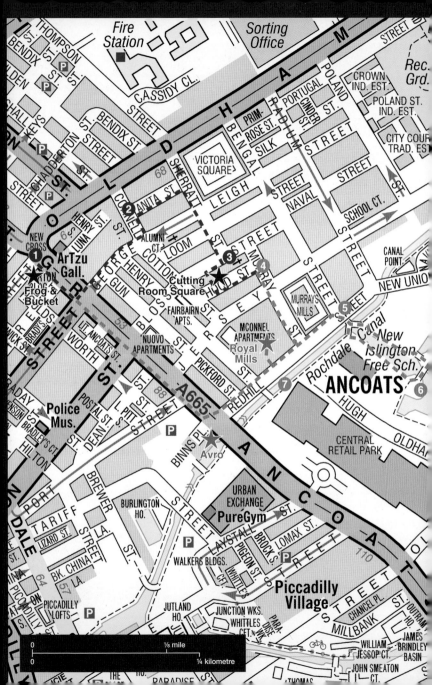

1 Start at the junction of Oldham Street and Great Ancoats Street at The Frog & Bucket Comedy Club ★. This sports perhaps the funniest blue plaque in the city, reading 'In memory of all the comedians who died on stage'. The club, established in 1994, helped make the career of comedians such as Peter Kay and John Bishop. Over the road is The Crown & Kettle pub sporting huge dangling 19th-century gasoliers. With your back to the Frog & Bucket, turn right to the junction with Lever Street. On your left, across Great Ancoats Street, is the 1939 Daily Express Building designed by Sir Owen Williams for the newspaper, now general offices. This Grade II listed Art Deco building in the 'streamline moderne' style is all about movement and panache. It might be from the 1930s but it looks more modern than most recent Manchester buildings. Cross Great Ancoats Street at the lights then follow the side of the Express Building to Cornell Street and turn left.

2 Take the first right into Anita Street to see the last remaining terraced houses in the city centre. They were built by Manchester Corporation in the 1890s as was the large tenement block called Victoria Square, now sheltered accommodation, at the end of the street. Anita Street was formerly Sanitary Street, marking the work of the Manchester and Salford Sanitary Association. The residents didn't like that so the 's' and the 'ry' were ditched to leave 'Anita'. Walk the length of Anita Street and then turn right on Sherratt Street, heading for the tower of St Peter's Church.

3 At the church, turn right into Cutting Room Square ★. This is the heart of Ancoats, which has been called 'the first industrial suburb'. The industry has gone and Ancoats is now a place of apartments, restaurants and bars. Cutting Room Square features tall monoliths with sepia images of ruined mill interiors from when the area was derelict. Hallé St Peter's utilizes the shell of St Peter's Church and is a permanent rehearsal and performance space for the Hallé orchestra and its choirs. The church is from 1859 by Isaac Holden, while the award-winning extension on the square from 2019 is by Stephenson Hamilton Risley and complements the older structure beautifully. Cross to the monoliths, turn left up Hood Street and walk to the end.

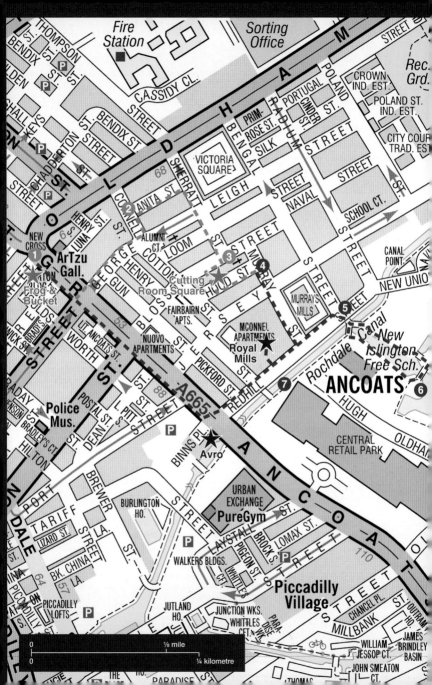

4 Turn right down Murray Street. Further along, the large gateway on the left punctures the impressive brick wall of the former and mighty factory complex called Murrays Mills. This is one of several surviving spinning factory concerns that defined the area. Now apartments, parts of the complex here date back to 1798. Continue down Murray Street and turn left on Redhill Street to Bengal Street. While Birmingham had its Peaky Blinders, the Mancunian equivalents were called Scuttlers and one of the most notorious gangs was based here, named the Bengal Tigers after Bengal Street.

5 Cross Redhill Street and go straight over the Rochdale Canal on the right-hand footbridge to New Islington. With the school on your right, follow the canal path to Cotton Field Park. New Islington began life as a Millennium Village in the early noughties and has now developed into a lively area of apartments, houseboats and food and drink outlets. The canal arm here is not original but adds character.

6 Cross left over the canal arm at the park and then go left, returning over the footbridge to Redhill Street. Turn left down Redhill Street keeping the Rochdale Canal, which opened in 1804, on your left until you see an arch on your right in the former factory wall. Enter through this arch into Royal Mills ★ . Go through the glass doors (permanent public access) and turn right into the glazed courtyard. These impressive mills were built for McConnel & Kennedy and are now offices, apartments and a coffee shop. French writer Alexis de Toqueville described these factories in the 1830s: '1,500 workers, labouring 69 hours a week … three-quarters of the workers in [the] factory are women and children.' To visitors, the scale and often inhuman nature of the new industrial process was something far beyond their range of experience.

7 Leave the complex the same way you entered and turn right down Redhill Street to Great Ancoats Street. Across the road is Brownsfield Mill from 1825. The building is now Avro apartments ★ . It was in the basement here that A.V. Roe (Lancaster Bombers and more) created Britain's first aircraft factory from 1910 to 1913. The building also hosted the Pall Mall rent collection company. Artist L. S. Lowry was an employee and would take advantage of his trips to the poorer areas of the city to sketch the industrialized scenes for which he became so famous. Turn right at Great Ancoats Street to return to the start point at the Frog & Bucket.

Az walk twelve

A Salford Stroll

Green spaces, the River Irwell and
19th-century buildings.

This is a fresh air walk with large portions of the trip taking place in green spaces. The Meadow and Peel Park are contrasting open areas: the former is informal, resembling a country park in the heart of the city, the latter is a formal space with pretty flower beds. Both are made more attractive by being bordered by the River Irwell.

This circular walk takes place in Salford, Manchester's smaller sister city, and delivers huge variety in both landscape and architecture. Salford was given city status in 1926 and has its own pioneering and proud history. At the beginning of this walk, in Bexley Square, there is an artwork that lists much of this achievement as well as naming some of the individuals that have given Salford such a rich and entertaining story.

The tour takes in a couple of fine churches, one, St Philip, from a nationally famous architect. The Crescent area around this church used to be very well-to-do then fell on hard times but is now undergoing a rapid revival as a popular central area to live. Restaurants and cafés are opening as a result of this influx of new residents.

The start point of this walk is about three-quarters of a mile (1 km) from the centre of Manchester and is a short walk from Salford Central Railway Station. There is a regular bus service between Manchester and nearby Salford Cathedral.

start / finish	Bexley Square, Chapel Street
nearest postcode	M3 6DB
distance	3 miles / 4.7 km
time	1 hour 45 minutes
terrain	Paved roads, some uneven paths. Steps.

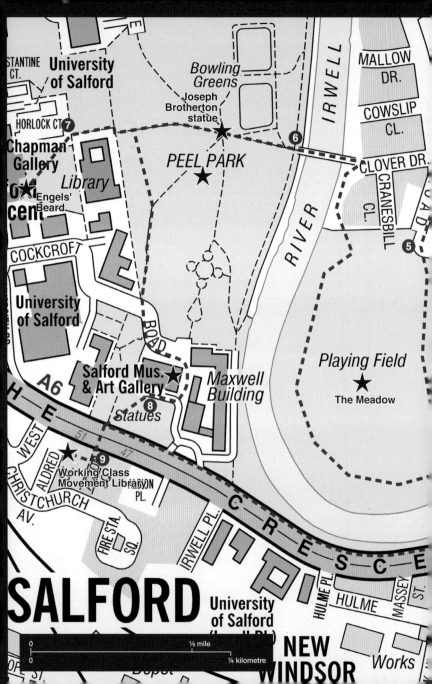

Adelphi Foot Bri.

CHIFFON WY.

BROCADE

ANGORA

A5066

BRAMALL CT.

MIST... STREET

LETOE GR.

NORTH HILL ST.

The Fria... Prim. Sc...

LINEN CT.

4

BLACKBURN

CALICO CL.

CALICO CL.

CALICO CL.

MATTHIAS CT.

ADELPHI CT.

BRIGGS ST.

MOUNT

WELLI...

ST...

TU...

SILK STREET

NORTH

DAMASK AV.

CANNON

ALLENDALE WALK

ARLINGTON ST.

BARNET DR.

RC Prim. Sch.

LOCKETT...

ADELPHI WHARF

BURTON WLK.

RICHMOND CT.

GEORGE

University of Salford

TRINITY GDNS.

BROTHERTON DR.

TYSO...

GDS...

KAYS...

GDNS

Weir

PERU ST.

MAYAN

HULL SQ.

DUN CL.

DEVINE CL.

STREET

SIMMS CL.

SOUTHWORTH CT.

AV.

ROSAMO...

STRE...

CLEMINSON

ST.

CLEMINSON

BROWNING

...versity ...alford (...phi Ho.)

ADELPHI

THE OLD COURT HO.

...OMBE PL.

ENC.

BANK PL.

WILTON PL.

ST. PHILIP'S SQUARE

3

TRINITY CT.

ST.

MELVILLE ST.

ST. JOHNS SQ.

CENTRAL CT. APTS.

former Town Hall

FORD ST.

BEXLEY SQ.

1

PL.

THE ROYAL

BANK ST.

GT. GEORGE ST.

TIMEKEEPERS SQ.

Salford RC Cath.

ST.

PHILIP'S ST.

CHAPEL

2

230

13

A D

WMROE ST.

VIMTO GARDENS

BAR...ROW

WAY

ISLINGTON

...TON S.

ISLING...

NEY S.

SID-

STAR DR.

Islington Park

CLERMONT W.

FACTORY

...LA...

JAMES

...BS ST.

NORTH

REFLY CL.

ROCKET WY.

LARK

WOOD...

CORNWALL HO.

STREET

...orks

CANON HUSSEY CT.

STR...

AV.

RODNEY ST.

LAN...

❶ Start at Bexley Square, off Chapel Street, in Salford. The columned building at the northern end is now apartments but used to be Salford Town Hall ★ . It was completed in 1827 as a market hall, became the town hall in 1835 and later served as magistrates courts. There were protests here in 1931 during the Great Depression. The main protest, nicknamed the Battle of Bexley Square, features in Walter Greenwood's novel, *Love on the Dole*. There's an interesting bronze by Emma Rodgers in the square, of a horse and a lamppost, featuring Salford 'firsts' and heroes. With your back to the Town Hall, turn right on Chapel Street and walk the short distance to Salford Cathedral ★ .

❷ The Roman Catholic Cathedral of St John the Evangelist was completed in 1848. Designed by Matthew Ellison Hadfield, it has an elegant, landmark spire 240 feet (73 metres) tall. If it is open it is worth a look inside. After the cathedral, turn right down Great George Street, then left along the pedestrianized St Philip's Square and walk to the rear of St Philip's Church. St Philip's Square is occupied by the multi-award-winning pale-brick Timekeepers Square development of townhouses, from 2017 by Buttress architects. The large iron artwork of a sycamore seed at the far end, by Andrew McKeown from 2002, points to the redevelopment of the area. St Philip's Church dates from 1824 and was designed by Robert Smirke

when this area of Salford was very fashionable. (He was also the designer of the British Museum in London.) The best view of the church is from St Philip's Place, round the left-hand side.

❸ Back at the sycamore seed artwork, facing the church, turn right and then left and then right into Encombe Place, past the former Court House of 1865. Turn left into Cleminson Street and then right into Adelphi Street. Follow this street down the hill for 350 yards (320 metres), turning left into Blackburn Street and left into Linen Court, to the footbridge over the river.

❹ Walk onto the iron footbridge. Looking south along the River Irwell you will see the impressive weir ★ , creating a broad waterfall across the river's full width. This was constructed in the 1790s to help drive a waterwheel for the silk mills of James Ackers. Cross the bridge and turn left into the street called Riverside, then left again on Meadow Road, which leads to a large open space.

❺ This green space is known simply as The Meadow ★ . This is not a formal park and comes with lots of wildlife and ponds, its border defined by a long meander of the River Irwell. It was early in the 1800s that the ancestor of Lancashire County Cricket Club, the Aurora cricket club, would meet at dawn to play here. Walk round The Meadow following the river path clockwise; with a circuit almost complete, leave The Meadow on the riverside path on the other side from where you entered. Walk to another iron footbridge over the Irwell and cross into Peel Park ★ .

6 Peel Park was one of three parks in Salford and Manchester opened on the same day in 1846, an early example of a municipal park. It has recently had a charming upgrade to make it a lovely place to spend some time. Walk forwards to a bronze statue of Joseph Brotherton (1783–1857), the factory reformer and campaigner against the death penalty and slavery. He was a vegetarian and agitated for non-denominational education. Continue away from the bridge towards the steps and ascend these, turning left into the area in front of the library building (alternatively, from the statue take the path to the right of the path leading to the steps and climb the slope via the ramp, turning left at the top). Take these steps and continue forwards along the side of the library building.

7 Head towards the building opposite the library, where there is a sculpture next to the gap through the building. This sculpture – *Engels' Beard* ★ – is not only an artwork but a climbing wall. It is by Jai Redmond and takes the form of Friedrich Engels' head. This marks the 22 years the German co-author of *The Communist Manifesto* spent in Salford and Manchester. It is an amusing and strange work and if you're feeling fit, have a climb. Retrace your

steps into Peel Park and at the bottom of the steps, turn right and walk to the long stairs under the older buildings. Climb these to Salford Museum and Art Gallery ★ and walk round to the front of the building.

8 This building grew out of a former mansion called Lark Hill Place. It hosted in 1850 the first true municipal library in the country. The building has been extended and developed many times. Sharing the western side of the space in front of the museum and art gallery is the former Royal Technical Institute, built in 1896 in terracotta, with some fine sculptural details. This is now a faculty of the University of Salford, which was founded in 1967. Walk to the main road, The Crescent, and cross at the pedestrian crossing to the right.

9 Turn right to see the Working Class Movement Library ★ , which occupies a former nurses' home from 1897. It contains several treasures over three floors and is an intriguing place to visit. Cross back over The Crescent and turn right. Follow the Crescent into Chapel Street and then back to Bexley Square (approximately ½ mile / 1 km). As you walk there is a good terrace of late Georgian houses on the right-hand side and, after Adelphi Street, on the left, the former Royal Salford Hospital, with its melancholy wall plaque commemorating the 14 nurses who died in 1941 during a bombing raid.

ᴀ̶z walk thirteen

Saints, Artists and Acid Rain

Manchester Metropolitan University.

This walk covers much of the area occupied by Manchester Metropolitan University (MMU) and also visits possibly the largest university building in the UK. This opened in 2022 and is the engineering campus of the University of Manchester. The building is astonishing in scale, for the number of its students and staff and for the research it can undertake.

You start the tour in one pocket park before looking at a fine example of modern architecture and then taking a spin to another pocket park. En route you discover the origin of a famous term. The walk is underpinned by always busy and lively Oxford Road which includes, as part of its scene, several very established businesses involving music and food.

The tour includes reference to the last Nobel prize winners from Manchester plus a pair of artists who did much to represent Manchester and the region graphically. It finishes with a look at a handsome columned building, scene of a meeting which had great significance for the destiny of Africa.

The walk is flat geographically but full of incident historically and rich with a variety of architecture.

start / finish	All Saints Park, Oxford Road
nearest postcode	M15 6BW
distance	1¼ miles / 2 km
time	1 hour
terrain	Paved roads and paths.

1 Start in the centre of the small but handsome All Saints Park ★ , off Oxford Road. As with so many pocket parks in Manchester this began life as a churchyard, around All Saints Church, which was destroyed in the Second World War. With your back to Oxford Road, exit the park on the Lower Ormond Street side. Directly over the road is the modernist St Augustine Church by Desmond Williams from 1968, the previous St Augustine again destroyed by bombing. Inside is the huge and superb *Christ in Majesty* by Robert Brumby. Almost next door is a surviving 1831 townhouse, now part of Manchester Metropolitan University (MMU). This was the home of the Bellhouse family, iron founders and building contractors. The Bellhouse company also pioneered flatpack corrugated iron houses which could be constructed quickly and easily and were used on such occasions as the Australian goldrush. Facing the house, turn right and then right again around the northern end of the square towards Oxford Road, passing a blue plaque on the wall.

2 This plaque on the MMU Building marks the work of Robert Angus Smith, a chemist. It was in 1852 that Smith put two words together for the first time. His observations in atmospheric precipitation in northern English towns and cities were responsible, he said, for huge quantities of coal-rich sulphur in the air, or as he called it, 'acid rain'. Turn left on Oxford Road and cross at the lights. Continue left down Oxford Road under the Mancunian Way motorway and turn right into Brancaster Road and then left into Symphony Park ★ .

3 Symphony Park is surrounded by the tall buildings of Circle Square. It was the site of the BBC North Studios for many years and the name refers to the location being the former home of the BBC Philharmonic orchestra. Retrace your steps to Brancaster Road, turn right and then left up Oxford Road to the unmissable Johnny Roadhouse store opposite All Saints Park.

4 Johnny Roadhouse store has been here since 1955, named after the man who opened it. Roadhouse was a session saxophonist who knew all the greats of the Fifties and Sixties. Paul McCartney, The Smiths and Oasis have all been customers at the store. A near neighbour is Eighth Day which opened in 1970 and is the oldest vegetarian business in the city. Greater Manchester has been home to the Vegetarian Society from its creation in the 1840s. Continue south, away from the Mancunian Way, along Oxford Road and turn left down Grosvenor Street. Cross Grosvenor Street to the huge black building.

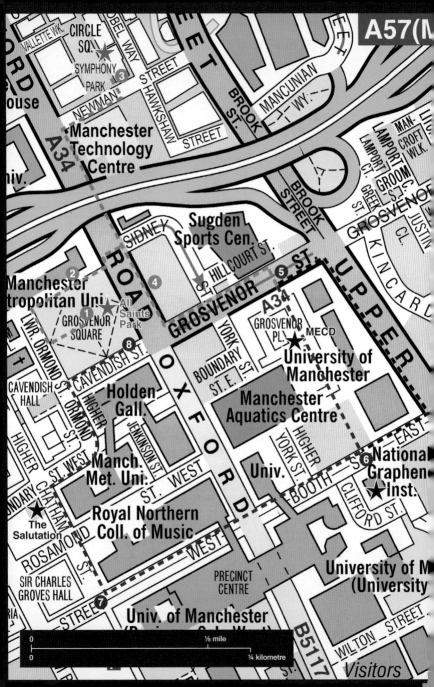

5 This is the MECD ★ , the engineering campus of the University of Manchester, which opened in 2022. It is 650 feet (200 metres) long, the size of 11 football pitches and has a student and staff population of 8,000. From Grosvenor Street, you can look into the High Voltage Room, where engineers make lightning. The architects were Mecanoo and during the week, the building is open to the public so walk all the way through to Booth Street West and turn right. If closed then continue down Grosvenor Street to Upper Brook Street, turn right, then first right down Booth Street West.

6 Opposite the southern end of MECD is the National Graphene Institute ★ , another building in black. Graphene, described as the 'world's thinnest material', was isolated and investigated by Andre Geim and Konstantin Novoselov at Manchester. They received the Nobel prize in 2010. Graphene has proved invaluable in a multitude of disciplines from electronics to construction and beyond. Continue along Booth Street West over Oxford Road, past the entrance of the Royal Northern College of Music.

7 Turn right down Higher Chatham Street and continue over Rosamond Street West, passing SODA (School of Digital Arts), with its striking digital light displays. At the end of the street, The Salutation pub ★ is a tiled 19th-century pub in the heart of MMU. Turn right along Boundary Street West, passing the School of Art's striking Benzie Building, from 2013, and then left on Higher Ormond Street. Turn right onto Cavendish Street, passing another building of the School of Art, from 1880. Artist L. S. Lowry studied here, tutored by another artist, Adolphe Valette. Valette, a Frenchman, captured the city's smoky atmosphere in masterful Impressionist paintings which can be seen in Manchester Art Gallery.

8 The next building, with tall columns, is the former Chorlton-on-Medlock Town Hall from 1831, now a facade for MMU's Mabel Tylecote Building, named after a prominent educationalist. In 1945 the fifth Pan-African Congress met in this building. Many famous names such as Jomo Kenyatta and Kwame Nkrumah attended and the event was chaired by veteran West Indian journalist and campaigner, George Padmore. One of the resolutions affirmed 'the right of all colonial peoples to control their own destiny'. The Manchester congress was the first real coordinated step to independence in Africa and the West Indies. Kenyatta hailed the congress a landmark in the struggle for unity and freedom. Over the road is All Saints Park, where the walk started.

AZ walk fourteen

Manchester Pioneers

The University of Manchester, The Whitworth and
The Pankhurst Centre.

This is a walk among the buildings of the University of Manchester (UoM).
UoM adds to the prestige of the city through its pioneering achievements
and its public institutions. It has provided an impressive twenty-five Nobel
laureates.

UoM also runs the fine Whitworth art gallery and Manchester Museum. The
latter is the city's main museum and is unusual among UK city museums by
being university run. This also means it is a research museum, fully engaged
with the scientific and cultural life of the academic institution to which it
belongs.

Also on this walk you will find one of the most impressive churches of the
region, the Holy Name Church, and, as is usual in Manchester, touch on radical
politics with the home of a well-known militant. There are, in addition, stories
of world-changing moments in science.

During term time the university adds energy to the city. It is one of the largest
universities in the UK, with over 40,000 students. You will find it an easy place
to navigate along what is claimed to be the busiest bus route in the country,
with plenty of cycle lanes and bikes for hire too.

start / finish	Alliance Business School, Higher Chatham Street (off Booth Street West)
nearest postcode	M15 6PB
distance	2¼ miles / 3.4 km
time	1 hour 30 minutes
terrain	Paved roads and surfaced paths.

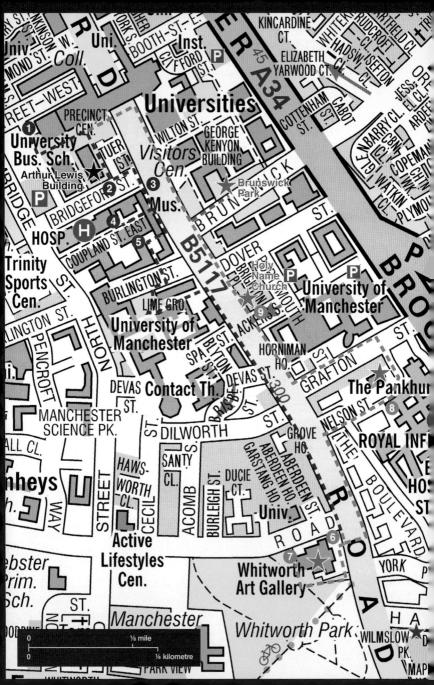

1 Start at the main entrance to the Alliance Business School on Higher Chatham Street. This is the second-oldest business school in the UK. Facing the building, turn right and then left along the south side of the building and pause with the Arthur Lewis Building ★ on your right. Arthur Lewis (1915–1991) was the first Black Nobel prize winner in an academic category, in this case, for economics. He partly developed his 'Lewis Model' in Manchester. The area here is called University Green. Pass the building and turn right, walking between the Arthur Lewis Building and the backs of the attractive older houses on Oxford Road, to Bridgeford Street.

2 A plaque on the wall of the building immediately opposite on Bridgeford Street declares this to be the building where, in 1948, Freddie Williams and Tom Kilburn developed the first computer with an electronically stored programme, called 'Baby'. Facing the plaque, turn left and then right along Oxford Road. Stop at the entrance of the Manchester Museum on the right.

3 Manchester Museum is particularly strong in natural sciences, geology and botany. It has a vivarium with live beasts and archaeology including a well-known section on Ancient Egypt. The museum was part of the original complex of the university built in 1888 but has been extended and refurbished many times, the most recent planned for 2023 with a South Asian gallery. Continue past the museum entrance to the archway on the right, leading to Coupland Street, and walk under it to the first building on the right in red brick.

4 This is the Rutherford Building, named after New Zealander Ernest Rutherford, the great physicist. Many discoveries were made here at the beginning of the 20th century, especially with regard to the nature of atoms. Amongst Rutherford's 'nuclear research family' were Hans Geiger, who would go on to invent the radiation counter; Lawrence Bragg, who won the 1915 Nobel Prize for his work on X-ray crystallography; Ludwig Wittgenstein, the analytic philosopher; and Niels Bohr, the father of quantum physics. Retrace your steps, turn right on Oxford Road, and take the next archway on the right into the old quadrangle of the University of Manchester.

5 The oldest part of the university on this site is at the far side of the quadrangle and dates from 1873. The style of all the buildings surrounding the quadrangle is neo-Gothic and most were designed by Manchester Town Hall architect, Alfred Waterhouse. If you get chance – during the week the buildings are open – take a look into the mighty Whitworth Hall. With your back to where you entered the quadrangle, turn left and cross Burlington Street, then cross Gilbert Square. Turn left on Lime Grove and right on Oxford Road. Follow Oxford Road all the way to The Whitworth art gallery ★.

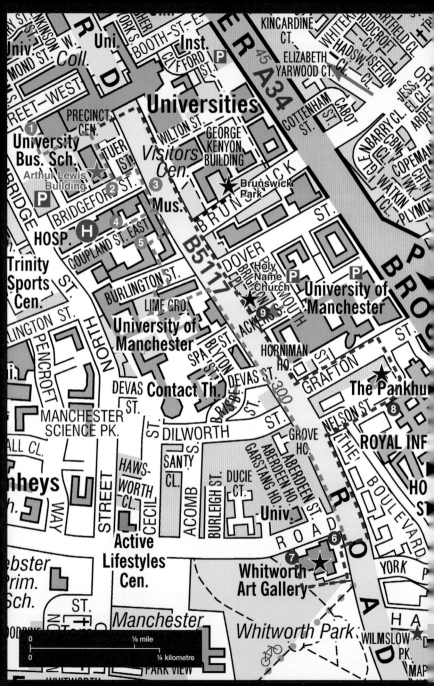

6 The Whitworth is one of the great galleries of Manchester. It's named for the man whose money created it, Sir Joseph Whitworth, the father of precision engineering and in particular, the universal screw gauge. The facade of The Whitworth is from 1908, a second phase is from 1963–8 and the latest from 2015 by MUMA architects. The collection is famous for its textiles, watercolours and prints from contemporary and classic artists. With the facade in front of you, turn left into Whitworth Park and turn right, walking round the building to the rear entrance.

7 This entrance, and so much of the newer building, stems from the vision of former director Maria Balshaw. She wanted the 2015 areas to almost merge with the park. The glass café, seemingly hanging in the trees, achieves this best. In among the real trees is Anya Galliccio's surprising and moving steel tree. Retrace your steps to Oxford Road and turn left, crossing at the first pedestrian lights. Continue left to Nelson Street and turn right to a pair of surviving houses.

8 One of these houses is The Pankhurst Centre ★, where in 1903 Emmeline Pankhurst created the Women's Social and Political Union in pursuit of votes for women. A militant organisation, it was nicknamed 'the Suffragettes' by the *Daily Mail*, as an insult. The women adopted the insult as a badge of honour and changed the pronunciation of the 'g' in the word from soft to hard, as they were going 'get' the vote, which was achieved in 1918. There is a small museum on site. Continue along Nelson Street, turn left at the hospital entrance and then left down Grafton Street. At the end, turn right onto Oxford Road and continue to the Holy Name Church ★.

9 The Holy Name is the finest Roman Catholic church in Greater Manchester and almost cathedral-like in scale. The church was designed by Joseph Aloysius Hansom and his son Joseph, and finished in 1871, although the tower was added in 1928 by Adrian Gilbert Scott. It's worth taking a turn round the church to view the splendid flying buttresses. The interior is gorgeous, very high and surprisingly light and airy. Hansom was also responsible for the two-wheeled Hansom cab. With your back to the church entrance, turn right and return to University Green, maybe taking a short excursion to the right into Brunswick Park ★ if you wish to add a short and attractive extension to the walk.

AZ walk fifteen

Sportcity

Gold medals and blue moons east of the city centre.

The 2002 Commonwealth Games in Manchester were a resounding success, with a million visitors, 4,000 athletes and packed venues. The games restored the UK's reputation for holding large multi-sport events and, as ex-athlete and leader of the London bid Sebastian Coe said, paved the way for a successful 2012 London Olympic Games.

This circular walk takes in some of the venues of the 2002 Commonwealth Games including the main stadium which now plays host to Manchester City Football Club. The stadium sits, more or less, over a deep coal mine which once served the heavy industry – engineering, chemical and textiles – that used to define this area of east Manchester and blight both soil and atmosphere.

As you walk through the area you will also encounter some interesting public art, a canal and one of the oldest municipal parks in the UK. There is a lot of new building taking place including an indoor arena, called Co-op Live, which has the largest capacity in the country.

The redevelopment of the area in the last twenty years has been nothing short of spectacular, turning a worn-out industrial landscape into a place of entertainment, leisure and sport.

start / finish	Etihad Campus Metrolink Station, Joe Mercer Way
nearest postcode	M11 3DU
distance	2½ miles / 4 km
time	1 hour 45 minutes
terrain	Paved roads and walkways, some uneven paths.

BROXTON ST.

Gas Holder

Philips Park Cemetery

River

PHILIPS PAR

★

Holt Town

P

P

WAY

A L A N — A6010

RTCITY

JOE MERCER WAY

Manchester Tennis & Football Cen.

P

6 SABLE

WILDALE CL.

WESHAM RD.

FAIRCL

7

STUART

DISH

CAVEN

ARCHER ST.

STILLWATER DR.

STUART ST.

Ve

THE CUBE

THE HIL

FRAME

National Squash Centre

1

Etihad Campus

STUART PL.

GIBBON

ST.

THE WATERFRONT

Excel Ho

Sportcity

2

Bradfor

Manchester Regional Arena

ROMSLEY

★

Manchester City FC (Etihad Stadium / Eastlands)

P

S.

Velopark

A662

SWALLOW ST.

286

3

Stadi

VIKING CL.

FAIRISLE CL.

BISCAY CL.

NEWCOMBE CL.

GREY

HOWARTH CL. DE

PNRWR CL. CL.

Sch.

HOPEDALE CL.

CLYDESDALE GDS.

SLEDMERE CL.

HAVANA CL.

KEY WEST CL.

VALL-EY WK.

CORLEY WK.

YEOMAN WK.

RAG-LAN CL.

PRENTICE WK.

ABERNANT CL.

DORIC CL.

BURNSYDALE WK.

GRIM DR.

REDFIELD

ROUSE

WILLOW ST.

ALBERT

ISCA ST

Sch

| 0 | ⅛ mile |
| 0 | ¼ kilometre |

Clayton

Bridge

Youth Cen.

BANK

BRIDGE

BANK

COMBE CL.

KEYN-SHAM RD.

PIONEER

PEN-RITH A.

OXENDON AV.

SEASCALE AV.

KINGSNEATH AV.

GLAMIS AV.

HARTINGTON

CLAYTON ST.

MARINA CR.

HURSTBOURNE AV.

HIMLEY DR.

GRANGE AV.

MIDVILLE RD.

GOL

STRE

EAST

BANK

ALPINE ST.

ILK ST.

TARTAN

GWELO ST.

STUART ST. E.

Sch.

RAVENSBURY

STOCK-HOLM S.

MIDLOTHIAN ST.

HEATHER S.

BEN ST.

RNLH S.

ILFORD ST.

ASH-HURST AV.

ST.

SUNNING-DALE A.

HEYWOOD

WINS-WELL C.

DR.

NEWHAM AV.

HMBRY FRN CRT

STHD

PL.

BURY THFD DR.

CRAVEN PL.

RHBKE SHFD

SENFIELD

LOWSD

RD.

HTN

STE

BDE

STREET

ST.

BMX Centre

⑤

JOHN ST.

BAMFORD

BUCHAN ST.

WEST ST.

STREET

COGH. FRND LAN C.

TRIMDON CL.

NAM DR.

THETA CL.

FLINT CL.

SWEET ST.

WHITELEY

BARRINGTON ST.

Rec. Grd.

CLAYTON ST.

CLAYTON HALL

Clayton Hall

★

④

Works

store

N E W

610

CROFT

SIDE ST.

CANTRELL ST.

AINTREE ST.

LINFIELD ST.

Clayton Hall

LANE

A662

ECCLESHALL

B.S.

L.S.

FDE S.

RSN S.

JOHN

WLM

AS

ST.

OLDFIELD

Works

E S

Manchester City Football Academy

Football Pitches

Clayton La. Bri.

TORNESS WK.

EMILY BEAVAN CL.

KINCRAIG CL.

BOB MASSEY CL.

STH

ootball Pitches

GREENSIDE

1 Start at the Etihad Campus Metrolink station and walk towards the stadium of Manchester City Football Club (MCFC) ★ . It is impossible to miss. Pass the shop on the left and take a look at the 53,400-capacity Etihad Stadium, as it is called. The stadium was initially built as the main track and field stadium for the 2002 Commonwealth Games. After the games, Manchester City Council let the stadium to the football club for an annual fee, and they moved here in 2003 after occupying their previous stadium at Maine Road for 80 years. Since then, the club has won the Premier League six times. The Etihad is now fully owned by the Abu Dhabi United Group. 'Etihad' means 'union' or 'united', thus MCFC play in the 'United Stadium', which could be upsetting for the 'Red' half of Manchester. Facing the stadium, turn right and after a few yards/metres you can't miss the impressive bronze statue on the right, called *The Runner*.

2 The statue is by Colin Spofforth for the Spirit of Friendship Festival at the Commonwealth Games. The male figure of a runner bursting from the blocks is much larger than life and surmounts a globe. Close by is a glass panel with the names of the winners of the various events at the Games. The buildings to the north of the statue include the National Squash Centre, the track to the west is home to a regional athletics centre. With your back to the statue, turn right to continue following the side of the stadium until you see the broad footbridge on the right. Cross over the footbridge and pause at its highest point.

3 There are good views back towards the Etihad Stadium and the city centre. Much of the site on this side of the stadium was formerly Bradford Colliery which fed a colossal, now demolished, power station. The mine workings were deep: 2,900 feet (870 metres). There is a memorial to the pit and the miners nearby. Turn round again and ahead is the main Etihad Campus which includes a training and academy complex for all Manchester City's men's, women's and youth teams. There is also a 7,000-capacity training and reserve team stadium (directly in front) plus an institute of sport and a sixth form centre. The 80-acre brownfield site was extremely polluted after years as a chemical works, and remedial works proved a challenge. Turn left at the training stadium and right up Ashton New Road, crossing over the tramlines and then left over the main road. Continue up Ashton New Road on the left-hand side and immediately after the large church turn into the small park to Clayton Hall ★ .

4 Clayton Hall, surrounded by a dry moat, is timber-framed and very attractive, a surprise in this ex-industrial location. The hall, which goes back half a millennium, is managed by an enthusiastic Friends' group and open on selected Saturdays between February and November (check the website). The church next door is St Cross, from 1866. The architect, William Butterfield, had a bit of thing for the brick and stone banding as seen on the church. Retrace your steps down Ashton New Road and turn right down Bank Street and then left through the gate in the high railings to the National BMX Centre and its shared entrance with the National Cycling Centre ★.

5 The older building, the National Cycling Centre, opened in 1994 and is said to resemble a cycling helmet. This has been a gold mine for GB sport. The national team, based at Manchester, has brought home 28 Olympic gold medals. The BMX Centre is from 2011. Both buildings have exciting interiors and are open long hours every day so pop in and take a look. The BMX Centre sits on the site of Manchester United's Bank Street ground before the team moved west to Old Trafford. During the 1894–5 season, Walsall Town Swifts visited and lost 14–0. They complained the ground was a 'toxic waste dump'. The match had to be replayed, not that it helped: Walsall lost 9–0. Facing the cycling complex, turn left and then right to walk past the main entrance. Bear left on Stuart Street and turn right into Archer Street. At the end, go left down Sable Way and right into Philips Park ★.

6 Philips Park opened in August 1846, on the same day as two other local parks in Manchester and Salford, Peel and Queen's. These were among the first municipal parks in the country and had been inspired by a pamphlet titled 'A Plea for Public Parks' written by 24-year-old Edward Watkin of Salford. Watkin became an incredibly successful engineer, especially of railways, although not all his schemes came to fruition. His determination to build a line from Manchester to Paris, through London and crossing from Britain to France under the English Channel, was started but scuppered by concerns the French might invade through Watkin's proposed tunnel. Turn left to walk round to the lodge, from 1868, at the entrance on Alan Turing Way.

7 Leave the park at the gate and turn sharp left down to the canal then right under the low bridge. This is the Ashton Canal, which opened in 1796 to bring coal into the city from Tameside. It is a narrow canal of 6 miles (11 km) in length. You will pass the Co-op Live Indoor Arena, on the left, with its huge capacity of 23,500. During matchdays the canal towpath is a popular walking route to and from the city centre, just over a mile (2 km) away. After walking under two more bridges, turn sharp right back up to Joe Mercer Way (named after a famous MCFC manager from the late 1960s) and the start point at the Metrolink station.

A⊿Z walk sixteen

Old Trafford and The Quays

Stadia, museums and media.

Say the words 'Old Trafford' across the world and many people will recognize the name from either cricket or football. The two huge sporting venues that both bear this name – homes to Lancashire County Cricket Club and Manchester United Football Club – are both passed on this spectacular linear walk between two tram stations.

The walk maintains its interest as it hits the Manchester Ship Canal. Grouped around the former headwaters of the canal are monumental modern buildings such as Imperial War Museum North, The Lowry arts complex and huge buildings occupied by the BBC and ITV television companies.

Popularly known as Salford Quays, the more accurate and official name is The Quays as the southern side of the canal is under Trafford Council's jurisdiction and the northern side is in Salford's. The scale of the area almost makes The Quays a secondary city centre for the region. It lacks the punch and vitality of the real city centre, as dock developments often do, but it makes for a fine walk. Dawn and sunset over the water can be exceptionally picturesque – the way the buildings are lit in the evening makes a stroll at that time a good option, though beware the wind that comes howling down the Manchester Ship Canal.

To travel to and from this walk by tram, purchase a ticket for Zones 1 & 2 from the city centre.

start	Old Trafford Tram Station, beside Old Trafford Cricket Ground
nearest postcode	M16 0HG
finish	MediaCityUK Tram Station, The Quays
distance	2 miles / 3.2 km
time	1 hour 30 minutes
terrain	Paved roads, some uneven paths.

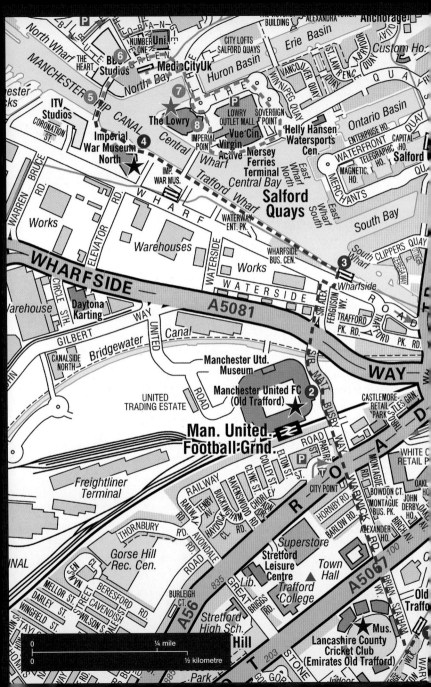

1 Starting at Old Trafford tram station, cross the tram lines to Brian Statham Way and walk to the main gate of Lancashire County Cricket Club ★ . Club cricket has been played on this site since 1857. After extensive recent renovations the ground now has a capacity of 26,000 as a cricket ground and 50,000 for concerts. Many memorable cricketing moments and many famous players have graced the ground, which often holds international matches with England. Continue over Talbot Road onto Warwick Road with, to the left, the imposing pile of Trafford Town Hall from 1933, with its central clock tower. Cross over Chester Road and continue to the main forecourt of Manchester United.

2 Manchester United's Old Trafford stadium ★ is by far the largest club football stadium in the UK, with a capacity of around 75,000. Above the club shop is a statue of the manager who made them famous, Matt Busby. In the forecourt there is a statue – *The United Trinity* – representing three famous players, George Best, Denis Law and Bobby Charlton. There is a memorial on the side of the stadium to commemorate the 23 people, including 8 players, who died in the 1958 Munich air disaster. United has won the league championship a record number of times. There are over 40 tours around the stadium and museum for visitors, who come from every corner of the globe. Facing the ground, turn right along Sir Matt Busby Way, cross over

the Bridgewater Canal, and then go straight down the slope of Sir Alex Ferguson Way, over Trafford Wharf Road, to the Wharfside Metrolink tram station.

3 From the western (near) end of Wharfside tram station there is a good view of the main ship-turning circle of the Manchester Ship Canal. The 36-mile (58-km) canal was opened by Queen Victoria in 1894 and was the largest British civil engineering project of the 19th century. It resulted in Manchester becoming the third biggest port by tonnage in the UK for many years, despite being so far inland. The impetus for the canal had been high port duties at Liverpool and harsh railway company charges, which the new canal bypassed. The canal headwaters closed commercially in 1982 when container ships became too large to negotiate the locks. Facing the canal, turn left to walk along the canal promenade to Imperial War Museum North ★ .

4 The Imperial War Museum was designed by Daniel Libeskind and opened in 2002. The unusual shape of the building represents a globe shattered by war. It is in three 'shards', Earth, Air and Sea, the three theatres of conflict. The disorientating nature of war is also represented with a complex and unnerving interior. Continue past Imperial War Museum North on the canal promenade, crossing over the canal on the swing bridge designed by WilkinsonEyre.

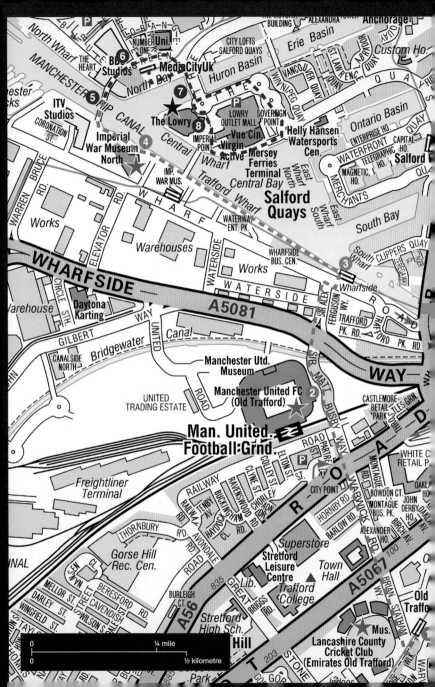

5 Pause on the bridge and look down the canal. On the south side is ITV Granada's headquarters and the home of *Coronation Street*, the world's longest-running television 'soap opera' which began in 1960. You can glimpse elements of the stage set of *Coronation Street* from the bridge. Tony Warren, who dreamt up *Coronation Street*, lived not far from here. Walk from the bridge the short distance into The Piazza at MediaCityUK.

6 MediaCityUK is a 200-acre development hosting key departments of the BBC including Children's, Sport, Breakfast, Radio 5 Live and several others. It also hosts the BBC Philharmonic orchestra. With the BBC and ITV Granada here, other production companies have also relocated or started up in the area. Walk through the gardens, which include the Blue Peter Garden that still features regularly in the popular children's show. The far end of the landscaped area brings you to a road called The Quays. Turn right. With the golden building to your right, cross over the dock arm.

7 This is Dock 9, the longest of the former docks and the location for brave souls to partake of open water swimming. It is also the location for the swimming element of the annual triathlon. Look carefully at the water and you will see bubbles rising from the deep. You may have noticed these elsewhere on the walk too. This was

an industrial canal so to help clean it, oxygen is pumped into the water. Facing the golden building, turn left to the large stainless steel-wrapped building of The Lowry ★.

8 The Lowry arts centre opened in 2000. Outside, it intentionally resembles a ship, albeit a futuristic one; on the inside it is all bright colours in contrast to the shiny silver exterior. The Lowry has two main theatres, the largest being the Lyric with 1,730 seats. There is an art gallery which always features work from the Greater Manchester artist for whom the building is dedicated, Laurence Stephen Lowry. The exhibition reveals how there is much more to his art than industrial scenes and 'matchstick men'. Facing The Lowry, turn left. Don't cross the footbridge (although you may want to walk over it and back for the view) but take the path to the left of the footbridge down to the promenade. Turn left for good views across to Manchester United. Follow the promenade towards the Watersports Centre but at the roundabout turn left, behind the shopping centre, back towards Dock 9. Turn left along the dockside, then right at the head of the dock, past the golden building again. Turn left to the MediaCityUK tram station, from where you can take a tram back to Manchester city centre.

⚿ walk seventeen

Grand Houses and Toast

The suburbs of Rusholme and Fallowfield.

A couple of miles south of the city centre lie the interesting suburbs of Rusholme and Fallowfield, both of which developed as separate towns until they were absorbed into Manchester in the late 19th/early 20th century.

This circular walk starts at an elegant 18-century hall before encountering one of the most unusual churches in Britain in terms of building material, with an interesting tale behind its construction. You will cross pleasant Platt Fields Park, skirting its boating lake to find a pair of curious relics lurking in a wooded area of the park, one of which is an ancient mystery.

The University of Manchester next takes centre stage with a charming and calming quadrangle of student accommodation. You will also visit another university-owned building, Uttley House, which has been inhabited by some of Manchester's most distinguished individuals. On the way back it's time for some toast, so to speak. On the subject of food, if you want to extend your walk there is lots of fabulous food available on 'curry mile', close to where the walk starts and finishes.

Wilmslow Road cuts this walk in two. Manchester claims this is the busiest bus route in the country, so getting to the walk should be no problem.

start / finish	Platt Hall, Platt Fields Park, off Wilmslow Road, Rusholme
nearest postcode	M14 5LR
distance	2 miles / 3.1 km
time	1 hour 45 minutes
terrain	Paved roads and paths, some uneven.

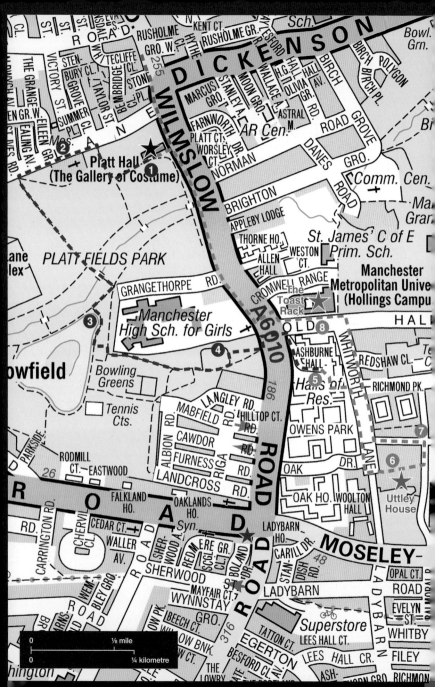

❶ Begin at the porch of Platt Hall ★ in Platt Fields Park. The architect John Carr's designs for this Palladian-style hall were modified by Timothy Lightoler. It was built for John and Deborah Carrill Worsley around 1763, in brick with stone dressings. Deborah's ancestor, Major General Charles Worsley, from Platt, was Manchester's first Member of Parliament (MP) and for a long time the last. In the English Civil Wars he was an ardent Parliamentarian, as was the town of Manchester. When King Charles II was restored in 1660, a vengeful monarchy took away Manchester's right to have an MP and it didn't get it back until 1832. Facing the hall, turn left through the park and take the first path on the right. Leave the park at the Platt Lane entrance and turn left to Holy Trinity Platt Church.

❷ Holy Trinity Platt is a real oddity, constructed from terracotta outside and in. Designed by Edmund Sharpe and opened in 1846, it was built for Thomas Carrill Worsley in a rush as he wanted to steal a march on his neighbour and rival, Mr Anson of Birch Hall, who was building St James' Church not far away. Holy Trinity Platt was one of three 'pot churches' in Lancashire which were part-experiment, part-advertisement for John Fletcher's fire clays at Ladyshore Colliery. John Fletcher was Edmund Sharpe's brother-in-law. Continue down Platt Lane, turn first left back into Platt Fields Park and walk straight down to the boating lake.

❸ Platt Fields Park was opened in 1910 by Manchester Corporation, now the City Council. This was a time of high unemployment and public projects were thought crucial in providing work. It took more than 700 men to turn the former country estate into a public park. The boating lake and island cover 6 acres and were the major civil engineering obstacle. On the left-hand side of the lake, take the path to the left immediately before the children's play area, heading away from the lake and towards Wilmslow Road. Just after the sunken gardens – Shakespeare Garden – turn left off the path.

❹ Hidden in the trees are Gothic arches which were once in Manchester Cathedral. When the building was being restored in the 19th century, parts of the damaged masonry were kept and they eventually ended up in Platt Fields Park masquerading as a romantic ruin. Running east to west there is a shallow depression on the border of the park here called Nico Ditch. This 6-mile (9.6-km) Anglo-Saxon ditch was either defensive or defined a boundary. It was previously much deeper and its exact date is uncertain, appearing somewhere between the Romans leaving and the Norman Conquest. Continue to Wilmslow Road, cross carefully, turn left and then right into Old Hall Lane where, immediately on your right, is a drive with a lodge building. Follow the drive round to the first house on the left.

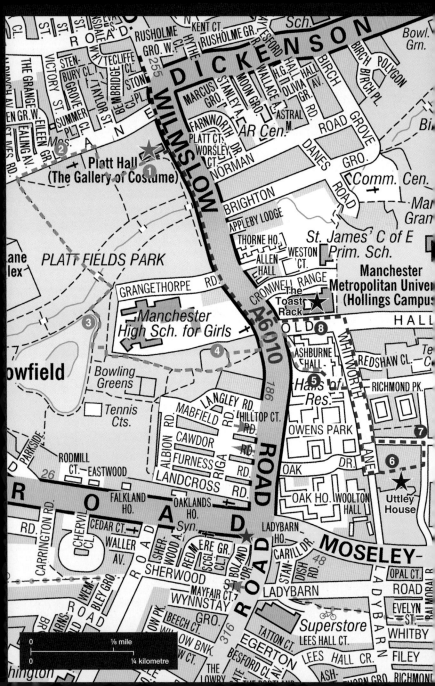

5 This old house is part of Ashburne Hall, a complex of University of Manchester accommodation. The house with its handsome columns dates from 1838 and was a gift in 1906 from the Behrens family to the university for women's accommodation. Textile company Behrens was set up by a German family of the same name who came to Manchester in the 1840s. The company is still going strong. Most of the buildings surrounding the grassed quadrangle are Arts and Crafts in style. With your back to the old house, head left, diagonally, across the quadrangle. Make for the small path that leads between the buildings and then keep left to Whitworth Lane. Turn right and follow the lane until you see a lodge building with a car park behind. Turn left into the lodge entrance, cross the car park and you are at Uttley House ★.

6 Uttley House (formerly The Firs) is an 1851 house by Edward Walters. It has been much extended and altered. The house was built for engineering genius Sir Joseph Whitworth (see walks 9 and 14). When Whitworth retired he leased it to Charles Prescott 'CP' Scott, who lived here until his death in 1932 when it was gifted to the university. Scott was the editor of *The Manchester Guardian*, now *The Guardian*, for 57 years and is famous for his dictum: Comment is free, but facts are sacred. Exit the car park of Uttley House opposite to where you entered and turn left up Chancellors Way to the roundabout at Gunnery Lane.

7 The Fallowfield Stadium lay close to this point. It was well known for its steeply banked cycling track and for hosting rugby union internationals, rugby league finals and a notorious FA Cup Final in 1893. On that occasion, 45,000 turned up to watch Everton play Wolverhampton Wanderers, and attempted to squeeze into the 15,000-capacity ground. Turn left down Gunnery Lane and then right on Whitworth Lane for 300 yards (280 metres) to Old Hall Lane. The playing fields across the road belong to Manchester Grammar School for boys – you can see the school away to the right. This is a 1930 building, although the school was founded in the city centre in 1515. Cross Old Hall Lane and turn left.

8 On your right you will pass the former Hollings College. It was built in 1960 by City Architect L. C. Howitt and is now Grade II listed. The imposing, tallest part of the building is known locally as the 'Toast Rack' ★ for obvious reasons. Opposite the end of the road is a cute former Unitarian Chapel called Platt Chapel. Turn right on Wilmslow Road and continue to the start point at Platt Hall, passing the attractive group of flats from 1939 called Appleby Lodge. If you walk just a little further north you can enjoy the food in Manchester's 'curry mile', an area of Middle Eastern and Asian restaurants and cafés, before catching the bus back to the city centre.

⚎ walk eighteen

Natural Pursuits

Moorland, wetland and woodland in Kersal.

Kersal has had a lively history since a monastic priory was established here in the 12th century. From medieval times the area has witnessed a variety of sporting activities, including one that was 'barely' imaginable. It has also played host to a mass protest, a daft golfer and a public execution. This circular walk starts at St Paul's Church, with its curious profile of two spires and its churchyard filled with the graves of brewers, scientists, poets and manufacturers, reflecting the 19th-century township's appeal as a fashionable residential area.

Although now a suburb of Salford, Kersal boasts moorland, wetland, woodland and a meandering river, making a walk around its edges a pleasant and interesting exploration of varied landscapes, with surprises at every turn. You will take an airy walk over high heathland followed by a descent to the banks of the River Irwell. This leads you to Kersal Wetlands, home to a variety of birdlife, where the views of the Manchester skyline to the southeast will remind you that the city is never far away.

Returning across an elegant 1960s bridge, the route takes you through the wooded area of Kersal Dale before the climb back to St Paul's Church.

Kersal lies 2½ miles (4 km) from Manchester city centre. Buses from the city stop on Bury New Road, close to the start of the walk.

start / finish	St Paul's Church, Moor Lane, Salford
nearest postcode	M7 3WX
distance	4½ miles / 7.1 km
time	2 hours 40 minutes
terrain	Paved roads, surfaced and rough paths. Steep ascent and descent. Steps.

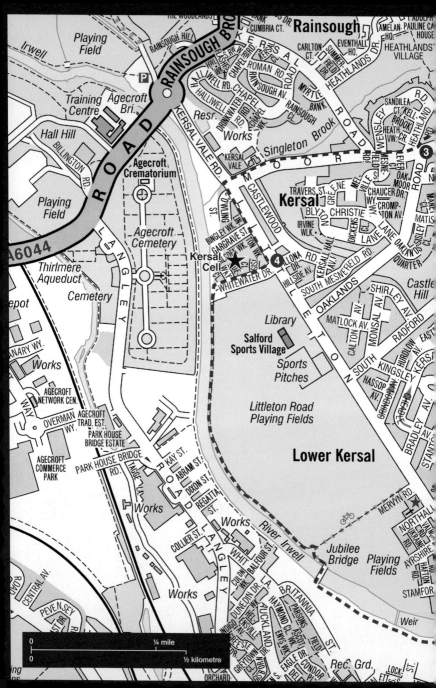

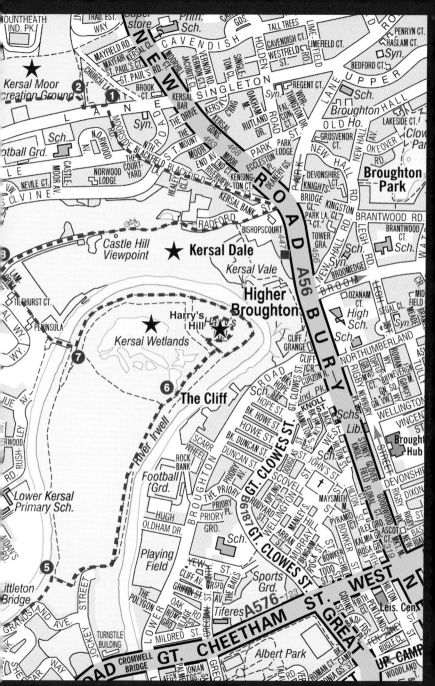

❶ Start outside St Paul's, 'the church on the moor', which was designed by Andrew Trimen and opened in 1852. A wander around the churchyard reveals the vault of the Holt brewery family. Holt's brewery is still thriving and still in the family. There is the memorial of Robert Angus Smith (see walk 13) and nearby, that of Edwin Waugh, a renowned regional poet. In the graveyard extension is a plot for the Cussons family, of Imperial Leather soap fame. Leave the churchyard and turn right down Moor Lane, then turn onto Kersal Moor ★ just after the graveyard extension. Take the left-hand fork and follow the path to the open area immediately after the copse of trees.

❷ Kersal Moor has a long history of sporting use. It was the site of archery butts in the Middle Ages and horse races from 1687 to 1847. The main horse race meetings took place around Whitsuntide and brought huge crowds, with over 100,000 gathering at some meets. A strange custom in the 18th century was nude male racing, an occasion, it was said, for 'females to study the form of prospective mates'. The moor has been home to the second-oldest golf course in England and hosted rugby union. It is presently the home of Football League club Salford City, with its 5,000-plus capacity stadium. Take the right-hand path through the moor, away from St Paul's towards the highest part of the moor, where James McNamara was publicly hanged in 1790 for a string of burglaries and robberies. It was also where a nationally significant event took place in 1838 when a vast crowd of Chartists gathered to demand electoral reform. Take the path down the hill, bearing left back to Moor Lane.

❸ At Moor Lane, look left and you will see the stands of Salford City Football Club. This was previously the location of the Old Manchester Golf Club. At one annual meeting in 1858, Malcolm Ross was the only member who turned up. He played the course and ate all the food. Follow the steep hill down Moor Lane for nearly half a mile (630 metres) and turn left at the roundabout into Littleton Road.

❹ Turn right onto Whitewater Drive and walk to Kersal Cell ★, a timber-framed house from the early 1500s on the site of a priory for Cluniac monks. It is reputedly haunted. Continue down Whitewater Drive; don't follow it right, but walk straight on, over the rough path, to the banks of the River Irwell. Turn left, with the playing fields on your left and Agecroft Cemetery over the river. Follow the river path for just over half a mile (1 km) to the iron footbridge. Cross the bridge and turn left, following the river downstream to Littleton Road. Cross the road and take Grandstand Avenue, which is immediately before the river bridge. Follow Grandstand Avenue into the wide-open spaces of Kersal Wetlands ★, a bird sanctuary and flood alleviation scheme defined by an exaggerated meander of the River Irwell.

5 Turn right, away from the river, and then left on the elevated path overlooking the river on the other side of the meander. The area became home to Manchester Races after their relocation from Kersal Moor until the last race, The Goodbye Consolation Plate, was won by Lester Piggott in 1963. Continue along the river path until you see football fields on the far side of the river. The fields are part of Manchester United's The Cliff training ground. No longer used by the senior team, this was where the famous 'Busby Babes' trained and, later, George Best. Continue the walk along on the embankment above the river with, on the left, a series of ponds, home to several species of waterfowl.

6 You will pass over sluice gates which can be opened to accommodate up to 140 million gallons (650 million litres) of water – enough to fill 260 Olympic-size swimming pools – during flood conditions. Further on, there is an obvious path curving up to Harry's Hill ★, the highest part of the Wetlands. The view from the top is rewarding. Before Manchester Races arrived, this area, known as Castle Irwell, had been the home of eccentric John Fitzgerald, brother of the more famous Edward Fitzgerald, translator of the *Rubáiyát of Omar Khayyám*. Descend from the hill and continue left, following the curve of the river meander for nearly half a mile (750 metres) until you reach the fine modernist footbridge from the 1960s.

7 From the embankment above the footbridge, the view southeast is filled with the impressive skyline of the city centre, 2½ miles (4 km) away as the crow flies. Cross the footbridge and follow the footpath straight on, with the blocks of flats on your left. After a short distance you will come to a large track crossing in front of you. Turn right on this track and into the pleasant woods of Kersal Dale ★. The woods here are very extensive, filled with all manner of flora and fauna. In the 19th century this was a favourite haunt of 'artisan botanists' from around Manchester. These were self-taught, working-class botanists and naturalists with other jobs such as weaver, shoemaker, blacksmith, saddler, mechanic, bleacher and twister-in.

8 Follow the path through the woodland for nearly half a mile (700 metres) to steep Radford Street. Walk up Radford Street to Blackfield Lane, just before Bury New Road. Turn left on Blackfield Lane to the junction with Nevile Road. Cross over Nevile Road to Moorside Road, which takes you back to St Paul's Church.

⚎ walk nineteen

Suburban Dreams and Delightful Gardens

The affluent area of Didsbury.

Didsbury, 4½ miles (7 km) south of the city centre, has a rich history and splendid parks and gardens. This circular walk takes in all these green and refreshing places, with stories to enthral as well.

Starting at the lovely library in the northern end of the suburb, the route swings south to where generations of wealthy Mancunians built their mansions. You will encounter a strange link to a mad television comedy show and buildings associated with deep philanthropy and social change. Didsbury was a place of religious colleges too but also of old pubs, and you will see both.

Then it is time to encounter Fletcher Moss, who did so much for this suburb of the city with donations of land which are now gorgeous gardens maintained by local volunteer groups. It is worth lingering in the gardens at any season.

The next destination is one of the grandest Victorian houses built in Manchester. This was the scene of an incredibly important decision which reshaped the geography of the northwest of England and had far-reaching economic consequences. The return to the start point is via another volunteer-maintained park, Didsbury Park.

There are regular tram and bus services between Manchester city centre and Didsbury.

start / finish	Didsbury Library, Wilmslow Road
nearest postcode	M20 2DN
distance	2½ miles / 3.8 km
time	1 hour 50 minutes
terrain	Paved roads and paths, some uneven. Steep hill.

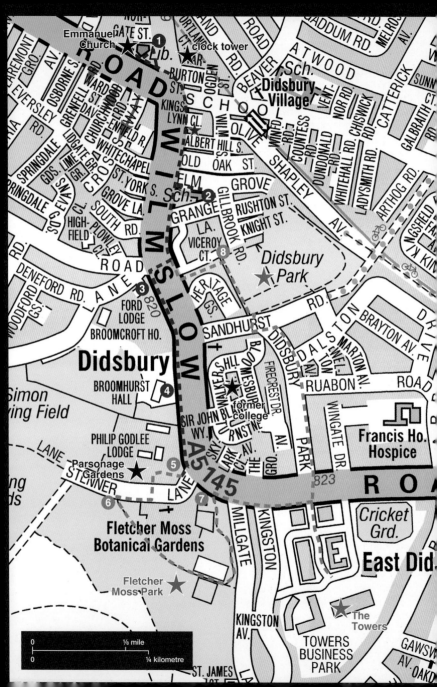

1 The start point is the delightfully flamboyant Didsbury Library, set back on Wilmslow Road. This 1915 building by City Architect Henry Price looks like a neo-Gothic jewellery box. It was funded by the Andrew Carnegie Foundation. Across Wilmslow Road is the John Milson Rhodes Memorial Clock Tower ★. Rhodes (1847–1909) was a doctor and a social reformer. Take the path to the left of the library to Barlow Moor Road and turn right to Emmanuel Church ★ next door. The church is from 1858 by Starkey and Cuffley. If you get chance, take a peek inside at the stunning William Morris window from 1889. With your back to the church, turn left and then right down Wilmslow Road, crossing Wilmslow Road to the left-hand side and passing The Royal Oak pub. The one-time landlord, Mr Webb, was a keeper of the monkeys at Belle Vue Zoo and once dressed a chimpanzee in school uniform and taught it to ride a tricycle, advertising his beer. When you reach Elm Grove, turn left to Didsbury Primary School.

2 The school is a very sweet Arts and Crafts building by John Swarbrick from 1910, with everything scaled as for children such as the little tower with its fancy cupola and children's faces on the rainwater hoppers over the drainpipes. Retrace your steps to Wilmslow Road and turn left, walking through the 'village' centre of Didsbury to the junction with Dene Road. Cross over Wilmslow Road at the lights so you are now walking on the right-hand side.

3 You pass The Limes mansion at this point, now split into multiple residences. One of the buildings in the grounds was home to Ade Edmondson and Rik Mayall while they were students in Manchester. Their time in Didsbury inspired them to write the anarchic 1980s student sitcom *The Young Ones*. A little further down Wilmslow Road is Lawnhurst, again split into multi-occupancy. This was built by Henry Simon in 1894. Henry's son, Ernest, was at one point Lord Mayor of the City and a progressive industrialist. Continue down Wilmslow Road.

4 Pause opposite the long and elegant Grecian facade in stone, part of the St James Park development. This building was the Didsbury College ★, a Wesleyan Theological Institute, now private residences. The former church that you have just passed was St Paul's and was built in 1877 to serve the Wesleyan Institute next door. Continue down the right-hand side of Wilmslow Road to the Ye Olde Cock Inn. The area between this and The Didsbury pub was the village green of Didsbury. The centre of the village moved north to the library area when the railway arrived in 1880. The lane between the two pubs, Stenner Lane, leads to the Church of St James. The gap between the pubs was known as the Gates of Hell. People had to avoid the temptation of the pubs before arriving at the church. Take the elaborate gate crowned by an eagle into Parsonage Gardens ★.

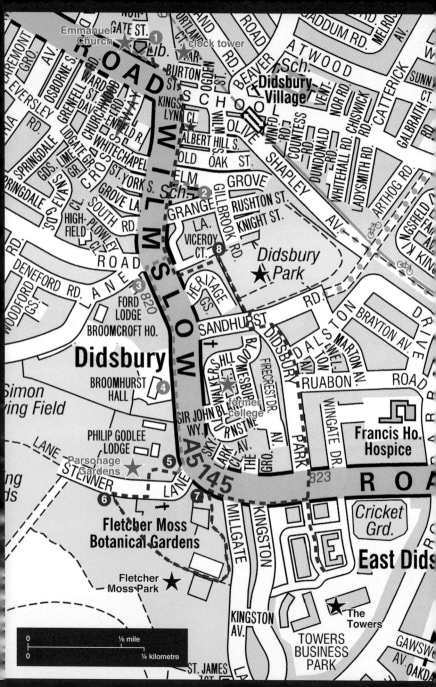

5 The gate came from the Spread Eagle Hotel in the city centre. Eccentric Didsbury resident Fletcher Moss brought the gate to the gardens in 1902 when the pub was demolished. Moss described himself as 'and absurdly antiquated author'. He lived in the Old Parsonage, the charming building in the gardens which are beautifully looked after by volunteers. The house, which dates from the 1600s, is occasionally open. Exit the gardens via the gate facing the church, walk straight across Stenner Lane and into the churchyard of St James's Church. St James's occupies high ground above the River Mersey flood plain. It is a pretty church with a medieval tower capped by strange pinnacles and loops from 1801. It now works with Emmanuel Church as a combined parish church for Didsbury. Leave the churchyard and turn left down Stenner Lane.

6 Take the first path on the left through Fletcher Moss Park ★. Keep left in the park, aiming for the tall brick park buildings. Turn left at the buildings, up the steep hill, to the terrace. There is a lovely view down into the rock garden from the terrace which, as with Parsonage Gardens, is beautifully maintained by volunteers. You might want to take time to explore. Both gardens were donations from Fletcher Moss. The building next to the terrace, a café now, was once the home of Emily Williamson. You will also find her statue close by. In 1889, Williamson formed the Plumage League in protest against the breeding of birds for plumage to be used in women's hats. This directly led to the formation of the Royal Society for the Protection of Birds (RSPB). With the tennis courts on your right-hand side, walk to Wilmslow Road.

7 Turn right and continue to the third street on the right, Didsbury Park, and turn right into here, walking between modern offices to the large Victorian house, now offices. The Towers ★ was designed by Thomas Worthington and completed in 1872. It is a crazy mix of styles and was known locally as 'Calendar House' as it is said to have 12 towers, 52 rooms and 365 windows. The engineer Daniel Adamson lived here from 1874 and it was in this house in 1882 that the decision was taken to build the Manchester Ship Canal. Return the way you came to Wilmslow Road and cross over to continue up Didsbury Park for a quarter of a mile (365 metres) to Sandhurst Road.

8 Directly ahead is the municipal green space of Didsbury Park ★. This is an attractive space so cut through here to the Wilmslow Road entrance by turning left to reach the park entrance then walking straight up the west side of the park. Exit to the left at the end, from where you turn right onto Wilmslow Road and retrace your steps through the village to Didsbury Library.

A‑Z walk twenty

Industry Turned Beautiful

The villages of Monton and Worsley.

This circular walk provides a woodland stroll, a remarkable delph cut into a hillside, pretty architecture and a return walk along the Bridgewater Canal. Every turn reveals features that tell the rich story of the area.

You start at Monton, 5 miles (8 km) west of Manchester city centre, at the Unitarian Church that has a surprising tribute to a scientist. There follows a lovely tree-sheltered walk along a former railway track raised high on an embankment. Drama is provided at the impressive red sandstone cliff face of Worsley Delph. Tranquil and pretty now, it is hard to credit it was once at the heart of extensive coal mines that helped drive the steam engines of the early Industrial Revolution in Greater Manchester and thus the UK.

The Delph is the where the Bridgewater Canal begins its journey to Manchester city centre and ultimately on to the Mersey Estuary. The half-timbered buildings that populate this part of Worsley are extremely picturesque but the colour of the canal water might be a surprise. You will follow the canal back on another raised embankment to return to Monton and the start point of the walk.

There is a regular bus service between Manchester city centre and Monton, and the nearest railway station (Patricroft) is just over half a mile (1 km) away from the start point. Alternatively, Monton lies close to the motorway network and parking is available in the village.

start / finish	Monton Unitarian Church, Monton Green, Monton
nearest postcode	M30 8AP
distance	3 miles / 5km
time	2 hours
terrain	Paved roads and surfaced paths, some uneven. Steep slope. Steps (optional).

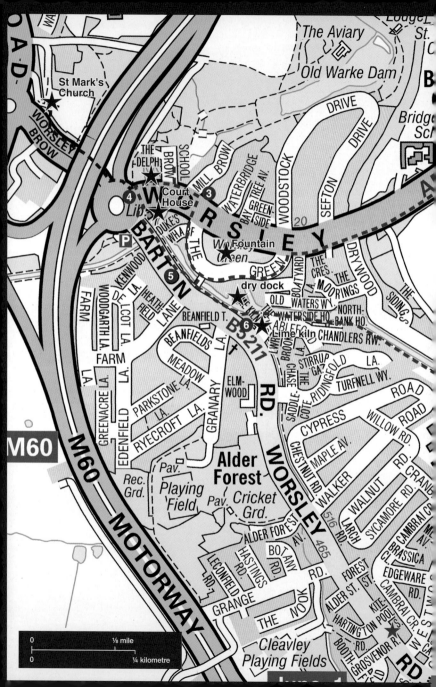

ROAD WORSLEY A57

RINGL...
ALLENBY R... RD.
LARCH AV.
LIME AV.
375
56
BRENT... WOOD AV.
...LEY DR.
...SH
...eph's ...ent
LANE
WELBECK DR.
...ad ...k ...er
2
BETWEEN 125
HANOVER CT.
CHATSW...
HOLTHURST
...CHWOOD DR.
...CHWOOD DR.
GROVEHURST
OAKDENE
FAIRMOUNT
MERE WOOD
RD. TOAD POND
CL.
BROADLANDS RD.
Sch.
MAYFIELD AV.
STOTT...
WOODLANDS AV.
ASHLANDS AV.
OAKL...
GBK
CA. G...
GAI...
RD.

BRAMLEY CL.
FAIRWAY
HOLLOWGATE
Broadoak Park
HADDON RD. RD.

HADDON RD. ROAD

Worsley Grange

SPRING CLOUGH
THE SPINNEY
NORTH
THE COPPICE

Sindsley Brook

LONS...
K...

Broadoak Park

WORSLEY GOLF COURSE

Bridgewater
...ER ...N.
...r Brook ...entre

GREENSWOOD RD. RD.
VERDUN
GREENCROFT
BROOK
FIELD

Canal

Dukes Drive Rec. Grd.

Brook

Folly

Brook

Westwood Park

CRESCENT

CRESCENT

RD... E

RYDAL AV.
MEADOWBURN NOOK

CLAYCOURT AV.
HAZEL MERE AV.

ROAD
MAY

ROAD

OAKMERE AV.
STREET

OLD FOLD

Club Ho.
CHURCHILL PL.

WOODLEAT...
STABLEFORD
GOLFVIEW DR.

Mo...

BROAD OAK...

1
MONTON GREEN

Comm. Cen.

WESTBOURNE
FURROW DR.
CLAUDE S...
LAMBTON ST.
ANS...
HAMIL-TON M.
HAMIL-TON ST.

DUKE S...

7 LANE

MONTON BRI. CT.
...ONFIELDS RD.
...ONTONMI... LL GDS.

BANK

CANAL SIDE
ALGERNO...

MARSDEN...
KIRTLEY...

...ERE
...BANY
...UGHAN SCH. S.
...Sch.
RD...

B5229

NAPIER GAR...
BRADFORD RD.

WATERFRONT ...HO...

MITCH...

PARRIN

❶ Begin at Monton Green, outside the Unitarian Church designed by Thomas Worthington and finished in 1875. Worthington designed many Greater Manchester buildings, including the Albert Memorial in Albert Square, later copied in Hyde Park, London. Unitarians have been known for their progressive ideas so the 1890s stained glass includes images of non-Christians such as Homer and Socrates. Look for the blue plaque on the church, celebrating physicist John Henry Poynting, born in Monton – craters on Mars and the Moon are named after him. Leave the church by the gate and turn right towards the roundabout on the main road. Cross Stableford Avenue and immediately on the right is a steep wooded path; walk up it. This is the former track of the Roe Green Loopline, a railway from 1870 originally built to transport coal but five years later open for passenger transport. It closed in 1969. After three-quarters of a mile (1.2 km) you will encounter the old platforms of Worsley Station. Fork right, off the former rail line and up Hollyhurst lane to busy Worsley Road.

❷ Turn left, walking all the way down the hill. After the row of old cottages, turn second left into a little road called The Green. Worsley Green provides a charming display of Edwardian Tudor-style houses, many with delightful Arts and Crafts details. In the centre of the Green is a curious brick monument called the Fountain ★. This started life as the base of a huge chimney when the whole of the Green was filled with workshops, forges and rail lines: the centre of intense industrial activity serving the adjacent coal mines. Follow The Green on its loop back to Worsley Road. Carefully cross Worsley Road and turn left to The Delph ★.

❸ The Delph may come as a surprise. This dramatic scene of cliff and canal waters is impressive but also played a major role at the beginning of the Industrial Revolution. Starting from the 1750s when coal mining began in earnest, Worsley was one of the hardest-worked locations in the kingdom. Coal was mined into boats in around 50 miles (80 km) of tunnels. Iron still leeches out, which explains the curious orange shade of the Bridgewater Canal water. You can glimpse the tunnel entrances at the foot of the quarried cliff face. The strange feature in the island in front of these tunnels is a modern interpretation of an 18th-century 'crane of curious construction, used for heaving the stones out of the quarry into the barges', as it was described at the time. The shapes in the water describe the mining boats that worked the area. Turn right on Worsley Road to the junction with Barton Road.

❹ The attractive timber-framed building across the road is the Court House ★ from 1849, built by the 1st Earl of Ellesmere for the manorial court. It is now a Village Hall. You can extend the walk by just over a quarter of a mile (500 metres) by turning right under the M60 to St Mark's Church (1846) ★ by George Gilbert Scott. This houses the Bridgewater Clock from 1789 which was formerly housed in a tower close to the Green. The bell still strikes thirteen times at 1 pm as the Duke of Bridgewater, who created the Bridgewater Canal, was worried workers would choose not to hear the bell if it struck only once at the end of their noon-to-1 pm lunch break. From the roundabout, follow Barton Road (left if coming straight from The Delph, or straight over the roundabout if coming from St Mark's Church) over the canal.

❺ After the row of cottages on the left, turn onto the towpath as far as the iron footbridge. Walk onto the middle of the bridge, which dates from around 1907, and look in the direction from which you have just come. The castellated building on the right hosted the Royal Barge when Queen Victoria visited in 1851. Through the trees to the left is the 1903 Bridgewater Hotel. This was designed by Douglas and Minshull, as were the footbridge and so many buildings in the area. Closing the view, north, is the Packet House with its jetty. This is where passengers for scheduled boat trips on the canal would buy tickets. Return down the bridge and turn left to continue along the Bridgewater Canal towpath. Just a few yards down the towpath you will see across the canal a still-functioning 18th-century dry dock ★ under an iron and timber canopy. This is thought to be the oldest surviving canal dry dock in the country. A little further down the canal on the right is a large mound girdled by an impressive stone wall. This was a lime kiln ★.

❻ Continue along the Bridgewater Canal for almost a mile (1.5 km) all the way to Parrin Lane back in Monton. The Bridgewater Canal began operation in 1761, transporting coal to Manchester about 7 miles (11 km) away. It was the first completely artificial waterway of the period in the UK. To begin with, the Duke of Bridgewater was laughed at for his enterprise and the canal nearly broke him with its cost of £200,000, yet just a short time later it was returning £80,000 a year. The success of the canal began 'Canal Mania' and the creation of miles and miles of UK canals. Engineers James Brindley and John Gilbert were responsible for this first canal and they made it the fastest in the country. There are no locks to slow the movement of traffic as the canal follows the contours of the land through the Lancashire and Cheshire Plains.

❼ On Parrin Lane, turn left and return to the start point at Monton Green.

credits